Fire Stations

Gerry & Janet Souter

BARNES
&NOBLE
BOOKS
NEW YORK

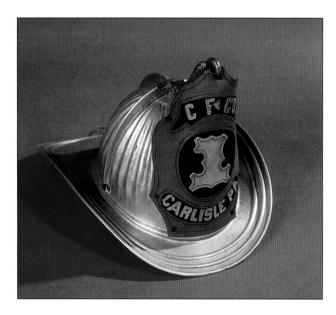

This edition published by Barnes & Noble, Inc., by arrangement with MBI Publishing Company

2000 Barnes & Noble Books

M 10 9 8 7 6 5 4 3 2 1

ISBN 0-7607-2061-4

First published in 1998 by MBI Publishing Company under the title *The American Fire Station*
© Andover Junction Publications, 1998

Photography by Gerry Souter except as noted.
Book design and layout by Maureene D. Gulbrandsen/ Andover Junction Publications, Johnsonburg, New Jersey, and Lee, Illinois.

Edited by Mike Schafer/Andover Junction Publications.

Library of Congress Cataloging-in-Publication Data Available

On the front cover: Part of the Galena Fire Department's modern equipment roster parked in front of the 1940 WPA Project fire house includes (left to right) a 1983 Pirsch No. 1 pumper, a 3-D pumper used for rural calls together with a tanker, and an Emergency-1 pumper with a 95 foot platform aerial. The quarried stone cladding the fire house was designed to match the dance hall next door—called a "Turner" hall by the German-descent population of the period. *Gerry Souter Photo*

On the frontispiece: Engine House No. 5, now restored as a museum in Allendale, Michigan, is home to this engine built by American La France in 1921.

On the title page: An alarm clangs and a Seagrave pumper leads the way off the ramp as the South Orange Fire Department swings into action. The gleaming engines and truck will return later to this charming, rambling structure that has served this New Jersey community well for over 70 years.

Pages 8-9: Rainwater from a central Illinois thunderstorm coats the streets of the village of Danvers as the town's firefighting equipment awaits the next call to duty on an August evening in 1997. *Steve Smedley.*

This page: An icon of American fire fighting, the helmet. This is the chief's hat from the Union Fire Company No. 1 of Carlisle, Pennsylvania.

Facing page: Two Chicago firefighters wearing SCBA (Self-Contained Breathing Apparatus) packs take a break after striking a neighborhood fire. *Tom McCarthy.*

On the back cover, top: An Ahrens-Fox 1928 piston pumper shows its "fighting face" parked in front of Engine House #5 in Allendale, Michigan. This excellent museum is housed in a rousingly ornate fire house built in 1885 in Grand Rapids, Michigan. One hundred years later, it was purchased for $1, dismantled, and moved to the Allendale property for reassembly. The museum houses a large collection of fire fighting apparatus, uniforms, and accessories in its restored interior. *Gerry Souter Photo*

On the back cover, bottom: The steam pumper from Aurora No. 1 that helped fight the Chicago Fire poses with the lads of that engine company in 1892. The firehouse was built in 1856, and it was from this building the pumper was dispatched, moving by rail from Aurora to the Baltimore & Ohio Railroad yard on Chicago's near west side. *Aurora Regional Fire Museum Collection*

Printed in Hong Kong

Acknowledgments

The authors wish to thank the following people for their generosity in giving their time, materials, and expertise to help us write this book:

Scott J. Beim, Green Village, NJ
Bill Bergin, Hoboken, New Jersey
Michael Boucher*
Ike and Tom Bozarth Jr., Mt. Holly, New Jersey
George Brown*
Capt. Albert Chandler Jr., Plainfield, New Jersey
Jeff DePilka and Chris Moelker, Allendale, Michigan
Karen Del Principe, Hudson, New York
Bill Frieburg and Bill Grant, Elgin, Illinois
Ben Gaskill, New Bern, North Carolina
Chief Ron Hamm, Fort Wayne, Indiana
Bill Hewitt, Aurora, Illinois
Deputy Chief Charles C. Kramer, Arlington Heights, Illinois
Eleanor Levine, Alexandria, Virginia
Ken Little, Chicago
Ron Manwaring, Murphysboro, Illinois
Ron Mattes, Mount Prospect, Illinois
Fr. John McNalis, Chicago
Dale Mygaard and Tom VanDokkumburg, Holland, Michigan
Fred Orendorff, York, Pennsylvania
Bob Peterson and Mike Rugh, Carlisle, Pennsylvania
Nancy Powell, Philadelphia
Jeffrey Radcke, Lake Zurich, Illinois
Rich Schneider*
Steve Smedley, Danvers, Illinois
Wilbur Tangerstrom, Racine, Wisconsin
Anthony Vecchio and Capt. Glen Savage, South Orange, New Jersey
Daryl Watson, Mike Simmons and Chief Mike O'Neill, Galena, Illinois

*Contributors to Ron Mattes' Firehouse Photography Collection

CONTENTS

A firehouse looks out at the evening street through big open doors. Chrome and painted steel and red glass sparkle on shadow shapes crouching inside. Firemen in blue shirts polish the equipment, or talk to passers-by. The smell of early dinner cooking seeps under the sash of an open upstairs window. The driveway is still puddled from engine wash-up every Sunday. Then an alarm rings and time compresses. Blue shirts disappear. A loudspeaker voice pipes out an address. Diesel engines whine-clatter-rumble to life, air brakes hiss. Street lights go red, halting traffic. Orange lights flash. Red lights flash. Strobe lights ignite the air with their rapid quicksilver bursts. A siren wail begins low and climbs to its ear-shattering ululation and down the driveway moving masses of glistening steel and chrome are launched, barking electronic blasts. In a few moments all is receding sound and the fire house is empty, silent, ready to be re-cocked.

Gerry Souter
CFD
Chicago *Magazine*

These men are the last American Pioneers, for they face, with each day, with each fire, an uncertain future... They are courageous without thinking about courage, and humble to a man about what they do.

Dennis Smith
Ladder Co. 17
Firehouse, *1982*

Preface

When Janet and I began this year-long pursuit of the American firehouse, we were neophyte fire buffs. Our qualifications were based around our two years of work contributing to and editing a history book, CHRONICLE OF A PRAIRIE TOWN—ARLINGTON HEIGHTS, ILLINOIS, and my background both as a writer and photographer for the past 20 years. For two of those years, I was a photographer for the *Chicago Tribune* and spent many nights and days shooting fire-scene pictures—ruining three sport coats in the process from smoke and water damage. We are both deeply interested in history, and now we had a unique focus in a literary area where the ranks of firehouse books are thin.

For resources, we discovered an excellent book, THE FIREHOUSE, by Rebecca Zurier, which became our architectural bible. She and her collaborators spent a great deal of time assembling an exhaustive look at both the architectural and sociological aspects of the firehouse. Without her efforts, our goals would have been much harder to reach. Next, THE VISITING FIREMAN, published by Steve and Lu Ann Hansen, became our guide to experts, fire museums and events.

In THE VISITING FIREMAN, we came across a review of Ken Little's book, THE HISTORY OF CHICAGO FIREHOUSES IN THE 19TH CENTURY, which led to our collaboration with Ken on the Chicago Fire section and all aspects of the early days of the Chicago Fire Department, including a huge photo archive. Through Ken, we were aided by some of his fellow collectors of rare firehouse and fire-fighting photography: David R. Phillips, Frank McMenamin, Bob Freeman, and Ken's co-author, John McNalis.

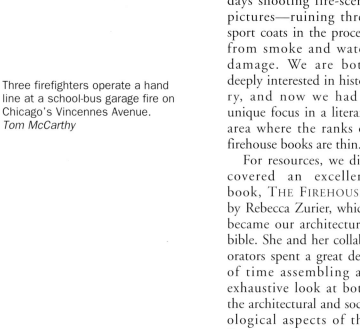

Three firefighters operate a hand line at a school-bus garage fire on Chicago's Vincennes Avenue.
Tom McCarthy

A casual telephone conversation with Ron Hamm, Assistant Chief of the Fort Wayne, Indiana, Fire Department, who is also a booster for that city's Firefighter's Museum, pointed us to Ron Mattes. A former fire fighter, Ron has images of firehouses captured on some 30,000 color slides. As it turned out, Ron lived less than a mile from us, and his expertise and guidance have been invaluable. We are grateful for his generosity in letting us use many photos from his collection in this book.

Tom McCarthy also came to us through Ken Little. Tom is a paramedic and supervisor of the Still Media Department of the Chicago Fire Department. His unique position allows him to keep a camera nearby and to "get inside the tape" at a fire scene for wonderful photographs of the fire department in action. His contribution to our book gives the Chicago Fire Department its due respect as one of the finest fire-fighting agencies in the country. Deputy Fire Chief Charles C. Kramer gave us great support with the Arlington Heights Fire Department. Within three days of closing our manuscript, he presented a proposal for a new firehouse to the village council and they bought the deal. He can now retire after 30 years of service with this achievement as a fitting close to his days as a firefighter.

Finally, our archival needs for the early history of firehouses and fire fighters were served by Nancy Powell, Registrar and Fine Arts Specialist of the CIGNA Museum & Art Collection. She was extremely generous with her time and helped us explore the considerable depth of this collection.

In our travels around the country photographing

firehouses and interviewing both active and retired firemen, museum curators and fire buffs, we were—without exception—received graciously and with enthusiasm. Though we read a number of books to prepare for our field trips, the "real world" of fire fighting and firehouses that these people shared with us turned these trips into treasure hunts. Every time we opened a door, we found new material and insights from knowledgeable and patient experts.

Most of all, we discovered a new group of heroes—today's working firemen. They don't wear their heroism on the outside, but carry it with them, naturally and with the confidence of persons who don't have to prove anything. They were unfailingly courteous to us and without their help, this book couldn't exist. Other firemen who have retired from the service—they are still firemen even though they've hung up their turnouts—also shared their memories with us. Men in their sixties and seventies lit up and their eyes focused

inward as they recounted stories and experiences that don't exist on printed pages.

So, here it is. We can never pass a firehouse again without imagining ghost images of stalwart men racing out the front door, towing a hand-pumper by ropes, egged on by their foreman, speaking trumpet in hand. We see plunging horses, nostrils flared, galloping down the cobbles, hauling a great smoke-billowing steamer; or see the gleaming chrome ball on the front end of an Ahrens-Fox engine as it wheels its fighting face around a corner toward the distant blaze. All firehouses, however humble or extravagant in design, are monuments to a breed of smoke-eaters, professional and volunteer alike, who look after the rest of us.

Gerry and Janet Souter
Arlington Heights, Illinois
April 14, 1998

With the luminous strips on their coats catching the light from the photographer's flashgun, these Chicago firefighters—using their signature snorkel—from Snorkel Squad No. 1 deluge a fire on Pulaski Road on Chicago's west side in the late 1980s. *Tom McCarthy*

Introduction

The American firehouse is a fixture in virtually every town in the United States. In some rural communities, it may be nothing more than a garage where the fire engine is stored. This practice harkens to our country's earliest days of organized fire fighting. The oldest firehouse in this book dates from 1798 in Mount Holly, New Jersey. It is a shed where fire buckets were stored and, later, where the town's hand-operated pumper resided to be called to action by the volunteers. Large cities host a variety of firehouses, each marking a period of development and growth, from the basic nineteenth century two-story engine house to modern concrete-and-glass drive-through facilities boasting the latest equipment and amenities.

The incredible variety of architectural styles—from beautiful and bizarre to profoundly mundane—demonstrates the firehouse's unique ability to function as both public building and work of art. At times, the firehouse must function in spite of these labels. At first, the firehouse was built around the equipment—a minimalist approach. Then, the firemen themselves expanded its role. Soon, it was a place to store the apparatus and a place to socialize with other like-minded worthies. Being a volunteer fireman became a noble aspiration. The nineteenth-century concept of fire fighting, its dangers and rewards for the public good, placed the fireman on a pedestal. What better way to express the importance of those brave lads than to erect firehouses that were architectural monuments. If public money was scarce, private purses were opened and an era of building splendid edifices dedicated to courage and grit swept into the twentieth century.

Socially, the role of many fireman changed from the noble volunteer to the paid professional, but this change was hardly a smooth one. The volunteers became political forces for machine politicians and their clubby competitiveness—who gets to the fire first wins—sometimes left the building to burn while the issue of who uses the fire plug was settled with fists and clubs. Then, the horse-drawn steam-powered pumper and paid professional firemen put an end to that nonsense after a decade of bitterness. Company by company, the volunteers in the growing cities were disbanded.

This transition is revealed in the houses that were built and rebuilt and torn down. The trend shifted from magnificent brick and carved stone fire barns to economical "storefront" houses that were punched from patterns and shoe-horned into commercial blocks. Two-story buildings, all seemingly cast from the same mold, were bricked or framed into place with bits of decoration troweled onto the facade. In 1935, during the Great Depression when cash was scarce, President Franklin Roosevelt's Works Progress Administration (WPA) was formed to put architects and contractors to work building public works projects, which included firehouses. In suburban residential areas, firehouses were camouflaged to look like homes with really big garages. No home owner wanted a public building dropped into his bucolic pursuit of the perfect lawn, flowered arbors, and shady elms. Gasoline power marked the next big change in equipment, making possible the architecture that followed.

Firehouses look like Spanish missions, concrete bunkers, art nouveau sculpture, French and Dutch chateaux, Norman castles, truncated skyscrapers, glass-and-steel fishbowls, Italianate palaces, Greek temples and featureless angled slabs colored with super-graphic letters and numbers like a child's playhouse. In dangerous neighborhoods, they are scarred with graffiti. They are galvanized metal quonset huts, wood-frame structures with false fronts, three floors of a parking garage next to a high-rise building. Some are just old buildings waiting to be put out of their misery by a compassionate swing of the wrecker's ball. They are concealed in industrial parks, combined with the police department, or they dispatch their modern equipment from lovingly restored Grande Dames built during the glory days of the nineteenth century.

Technology has changed the firehouse. Society's needs and demands have toyed with its function. And through it all, there has remained one constant:

the firemen. They have always represented the best of us, the voice in our heads that wants to say, "I'm here to help." Often, they come from families of firemen going back generations. They are ex-military people. They are adrenaline junkies. In rural communities, they are shop owners, plumbers, farmers, carpenters and bankers who put aside their tools or computers when their pagers beep or the town fire siren blares. They are also, as one veteran put it with a wink, ". . . crazy. A building's on fire and everyone is running out. And who's running in?"

If they are crazy, then the firehouse is their asylum. It's their home away from home, their office. It's the place from which they launch their attack, from which they jump into the unknown every time the alarm sounds. If there is a building that has a life of its own, it is the firehouse. The intensity of the lives lived within its walls becomes part of the brick and mortar, the old, dark wood, the concrete slab, the photos on the walls next to the framed badges.

IN THIS BOOK, we'll look at examples of firehouses that represent their era. We'll look at everything from the most simple lean-to in a field or shed in a graveyard to magnificent piles of architectural slight-of-hand and Victorian bric-a-brac laid on with a heavy hand. Between the stories of individual firehouses, we'll include some of the fire-fighting history that shaped their era. Some stories are about architecture, others are about how the houses were built. A few are incredulous about why the houses were built. Of all public buildings, the tasks required of a firehouse make it unique. The challenge of resolving those tasks has always reflected the time in which they were built. We can see our own quirks, foibles, and agendas in their impression.

To begin, we'll put the work of a firehouse in context. We'll start with a slice of history from the heart of America, a look at one of the great conflagrations of all time where men and horses and steam power fought from firehouses long since pulled down. It was one of the most-terrifying losing battles of all time—the great Chicago Fire.

Two firefighters in bas relief guard the main door of the Rochester, New York, Fire Department Headquarters in solemn dignity. Dating from 1936, the headquarters building, shown in August 1990, and its ancillary structures comprise a superb example of Art Deco design as applied to industrial use. *Mike Schafer*

ABOVE: A Currier & Ives depiction of the Great Chicago Fire shows how it might have appeared looking west from Lake Michigan. The fire has already jumped across the Chicago River (center of scene, emptying into the lake) and is working its way north driven by high winds off surrounding bone-dry prairies. *Courtesy, CIGNA Museum and Art Collection.*

CHAPTER 1

The Great Chicago Fire

THE FIRE TO END ALL FIRES!

By 3:30 a.m., October 8, 1871, the fire that had started nearly six hours earlier at the Lull & Holmes planing mill on Chicago's West Side had been reduced to a smoldering coal yard and some glowing embers in an area that had leveled four square city blocks. This blaze, the last of 30 fires in the past week, had involved the entire Chicago Fire Department.

As the sun rose above Lake Michigan, at the corner of Clinton and Jackson streets, a few members of the crew of the Engine 3 steamer, the *William James*, poked through the smoking ruins of the one-story frame storage garage that had collapsed on their pumper. Hose cart *A. Clybourne* and Engine 7 steam pumper *Liberty*, a reserve engine, had also been wrecked. Because of the intensity of the battle, many men of Chicago's total roster of 219 firefighters were now unfit for work.

Inside the Supply Hose No. 2 firehouse, the *America* hose cart leaned on its whiffletree (yoke). Its 600 feet of wet hose had been man-hauled by rope-and-pulley high up into the hose tower at the rear of the building to hang and dry; another length of stored hose had been rolled out and wound onto the cart's reel. This hose was battered and in need of replacement after the past few weeks of constant alarms. The fire department's request for 15,000 feet of new hose had been cut by 5,000 feet and every length was precious.

The large equipment bay with its 30-foot ceiling seemed empty since the steamer *Chicago* had been moved to a new two-bay house at 195 S. Jefferson Street. The remaining horse twitched with fatigue in her stall and gratefully gulped down water from her trough. Dave Manwell, the horseman, finished her grooming, coughed, and spat something black into a spittoon. He made his way upstairs on shaky legs to his bed in the dormitory.

A hazy Sunday passed and Charley Anderson, the driver, awoke from a fitful sleep to go up the street toward Harrison and Halsted for dinner and a "wee dram" of refreshment to cut the soot in his throat. Foreman John Dorcey left the big wooden doors open in the warm evening breeze, pulled a chair out onto the driveway, and sat down in his stocking feet.

At Engine 6—the home of the Amoskeag-built steam pumper *Little Giant* and its attendant hose cart—the crew was still asleep after they had finished cleaning the engine's pump mechanism, feeding the five soot-grimed horses, and trimming singed spots from their close-cropped manes. The firemen were red-eyed and coughing as they had made their way up the steep back stairs of the old two-story frame house built in 1864. Foreman Bill Musham was the last to leave the bay after writing up his report.

As evening approached, Joseph Lauf, the stoker, carried up an extra scuttle of coal from the basement and dumped it into the storage pan just in front of the *Little Giant*'s furnace fire doors. His shoulders ached as he regarded the fuel supply that would last just 20 minutes at a fire scene. He had drawn the night watch in the wooden tower that faced out on the jumble of houses and barns on Maxwell Street between Clinton and Canal streets.

By eight o'clock Sunday night, Lauf had made his way up the circular iron stairway, dodging still-damp lengths of dangling hose and managed to not spill a drop of the black coffee he gingerly carried in a tin cup. His view included a star-pierced sky blending with the dim flicker of gas and kerosene lamps in windows and on street corners. He turned his chair to face northwest where the coal yard of the Pittsburgh, Fort Wayne & Chicago Rail Road was still a red glow that would burn for days. The air was brick-dry and unseasonably warm for October; only an inch and a half of rain had fallen since July. The

Hand lanterns hung on the Elgin (Illinois) pumper *James T. Gifford*, one of many pumpers sent from outlying towns to help fight the fire that reshaped the city.

wood ledge of the watch tower was dry as tinder under his elbow. Seventeen hours of fire fighting without food or rest tugged at his eyelids. He sipped the pungent coffee.

At the new two-bay firehouse just completed at 195 S. Jefferson, Foreman Chris Schimmels watched engineer Henry Coleman check the grease and oil cups of the Engine 5 steam pumper *Chicago*. The engineer was shook as he examined the pump mechanism that had endured 17 hours of hard work after a week of fires. In the other bay, the men of Ladder Truck 2, the *Protector* —who usually didn't mix with the enginemen— knew there were problems with the steamer but kept their minds on their own routines. Outside, pipeman David Kenyon leaned against the brick wall, drawing in lungs full of fresh air. Even though the house was brand-new, its confines were already stinking of coal smoke, sweaty horses, and sweaty men, hay, hot grease, oil, and the ammoniac sting of horse urine. At least on the street, the warm southern breeze carried the stinks aloft. He was hungry, but still had hose nozzles to clean.

The firehouse of Supply Hose 2 and home for the hose cart *America*. Responding to a passerby's alarm on Oct. 8, 1871, the *America* and its crew were the first to put water on the Great Chicago Fire. *Photo by Freeman, Bob Freeman Collection*

In the alley behind Engine 5, the coal wagon's exhausted helper wrestled the long tin chute from its lodging in the opening above the firehouse's basement coal bunker and tipped it back into the wagon bed. All of the houses were short of coal and the wagons had been on the streets constantly for the past seven days. It would take a week to get all the firehouses re-supplied. He pulled himself up onto the wagon box next to the driver, rubbed his red-rimmed eyes with grimy hands and tried not to think of the next day's deliveries.

Five blocks away from the *Little Giant*'s firehouse, Daniel "Peg Leg" Sullivan was a restless man. He had a house in Conley's Patch across DeKoven Street from the house and barn of Patrick and Katherine O'Leary. He was a drayman—he worked with horse teams and wagons—and Sunday, his day of rest, was rapidly winding down. The sun had set at about 5:30 and there was no moon, so DeKoven Street was pitch dark save for lights from kerosene lamps in the open windows on this warm hazy evening. A party was in progress in the McLaughlin house that stood in front of O'Leary's smaller home.

Sullivan had visited the party, but only two tin "growlers" of beer purchased at Frank Shults' saloon a half block away were available to the guests for refreshment. Resigned to an early night, he crossed the street heading back to his own house. It was 8:30 and lively fiddle music came from the McLaughlin place. Instead of going into his home, Sullivan settled down on the wood sidewalk in front of the house next door to his that belonged to his neighbor, Thomas White. He could lean back against White's wood fence, extend his wooden leg comfortably, and light his clay pipe with a sliver of tobacco cut from a plug in his pocket.

From around the corner of McLaughlin's house, Dennis Regan, who also lived on DeKoven Street, approached. He had visited the O'Leary's, finding them both in bed, Mrs. O'Leary with a sore foot. He sat down next to Sullivan with an idea to buy their way into the party with a quart of milk from one of O'Leary's cows and some Irish Lightning that Regan had; they'd pay for the milk in the morning. Regan headed off to get the booze while Sullivan got to his foot and headed for the barn, which was behind O'Leary's house and hidden from view by the Forbes house, the Dalton house, and the Dalton's eight-foot rear fence.

In the moonless darkness, it took the peg-legged man some time to reach the barn. He traversed a narrow alley, squeezing past O'Leary's parked new wagon. The journey was tiresome and the barn was

pitch dark. He could smell the animals, the three tons of Timothy hay in the loft, the coal heaped in a corner, and the urine-soaked wood shavings scattered ankle deep on the mud floor by the stalls. At about 8:45, Daniel Sullivan struck a match on the door's wood sill to try and find a lamp. It burned down to his fingers. He shook it, tossed it aside and lit another.

Regan was crossing DeKoven Street with the half pint of Paddy when he saw blossoming flames. Sullivan, with singed hair and smoking shirtsleeves and carrying his unstrapped peg leg, hopped from O'Leary's barn hanging onto the neck of a bawling

calf. Regan watched the inferno from the blazing barn lash into the side of the Dalton house. He took a quick swig of the whiskey and ran to waken the O'Learys. He and Sullivan would talk later*.

In the firehouse watchtower of Engine 6, the flick-

*This account of the start of the Great Chicago Fire is based on exhaustive work by historian Richard F. Bales in his article, "Did the Cow Do It? A New Look at the Great Chicago Fire," which appeared in the *Illinois Historical Journal* (Vol. 90, No. 1, Spring 1997). His speculations are based on actual post-fire testimony rather than newspaper accounts and books that used those accounts. He also produced a map recreating the actual pre-fire layout of the O'Leary, McLaughlin, Sullivan, White, Dalton, and Forbes properties on DeKoven Street to debunk Dan Sullivan's and Dennis Regan's contradictory testimonies. While this speculation must remain just that, there is more evidence to support it than the story concocted by journalists of the period blaming Mrs. O'Leary and her cow that has been told and retold over the decades.

The men of Engine 6 pose in front of their wood-frame firehouse on Maxwell Street. This *Little Giant* Amoskeag First Class piston pumper was the first fire engine on the scene at DeKoven Street to fight the Great Chicago Fire that began on the O'Leary property. It was drawn by four horses and attended by a one-horse hose cart. *Frank McMenamin, DDS Collection*

er of flame caught Joseph Lauf's eye and jarred him from a half-doze. His chair tipped forward and he was on his feet.

"Turn out! Turn out!" he shouted down the stairwell. Seven men stumbled from their beds, groping for their boots. "Looks like it's four or five blocks north, goin' up Jefferson!" he yelled as he made his way down the spiral staircase toward the engine floor.

By the time he reached the floor, the four horses were being hitched to the steamer and the boiler preheater pipe was being disconnected from the firehouse hot water supply line by the engineer. The hose-cart horse whinnied as its collar was looped over its neck. Lauf swept up a handful of kerosene-soaked tinder and thrust it into the *Little Giant*'s firebox, followed by a lit match. Foreman Musham rapped out a "still" alarm on the telegraph to headquarters that Engine 6 was rolling to a fire in the West Division. The driver whistled, and Musham caught a grip on the engine's footplate as it rumbled past followed by the hose cart. The horses' hooves struck sparks on the cobbles as they broke into a full gallop down the gaslit street.

John Dorcey, the *America* hose cart's foreman, had been speaking with William Fraser, a baker, in front of the firehouse and decided to go in and fetch his boots. When he came back to his chair, Fraser was staring down the street. Fraser pointed, "Looks like a fire."

Dorsey followed Fraser's pointing finger and saw an orange glow in the southeast.

"By God, that *is* a fire!" Dorcey exclaimed. He and Fraser ran into the firehouse. While Dorcey roused horseman Manwell from bed, Fraser opened the stall door and the horse trotted to her place between the traces. In a minute's time, Manwell was at the reins with Dorcey and Fraser standing on the rear footboard. As the hose cart rolled out onto the street, the alarm was dinging behind them. But they knew where the fire was. At the corner of Harrison and Halsted streets, Charley Anderson, the driver, raced to the curb and jumped on the cart while Fraser sprawled forward across the reel.

A passerby stuck his head into the doorway of Engine 5's firehouse and shouted the alarm. As the *Chicago*'s engine crew hitched their two horses, an alarm came in: three dings, then four, then two 3-4-2 rings. That alarm meant a fire in the opposite direction to the one reported.

"Which one?" asked the engine driver. Chris Schimmels, the firehouse foreman, looked out at the night beyond the open doors.

The O'Leary property on DeKoven Street after the Great Chicago Fire. Everything behind it and to the north is gone. The McLaughlin house, site of the Sunday night party on Oct. 8, 1871, fronts onto the wood sidewalk. The O'Leary house is attached behind it. Here, Katherine O'Leary lay in her bed while "Peg Leg" Sullivan burned down her barn and most of Chicago. *Courtesy Chicago Historical Society*

The Jefferson Street house of Engine 5, the *Chicago,* and truck 2, the *Protector,* at the time of the Chicago Fire. The *Chicago*'s pump broke during the fire-fighting and was repaired on the spot; it kept up the fight for the rest of the battle. *Collection of David R. Phillips.*

"We'll take the one this feller's seen!" he shouted, and jumped on the rear of the steamer as it wheeled past, turning in the direction of the passerby's pointing hand. The ladder truck *Protector* followed behind its two-horse hitch.

The panicked passerby, unfortunately, was pointing in the wrong direction. The driver realized the error after having traveled a block, hauled the horses around to Van Buren Street, then west to Des Plaines Avenue and arrived, eventually, at a fire hydrant on Jefferson Street facing a furnace of fire and smoke.

Firehouses across the city threw open their doors as alarms rang and the fire boiled its way north. The *America* hose cart would arrive first in front of the fire, but its water pressure was limited to what came from the hydrant, forcing the men to fight up close to the blaze. The *Little Giant* was the first steam pumper on the scene, setting up behind the fire on DeKoven Street, but the winds blew their water stream to feathers before it could drench the burning houses and barns. Engine 5, the *Chicago,* arrived and began fighting the fire on Taylor Street. At nearly the same time, the *Wabansia,* another steam pumper, took over the *America*'s fire hydrant—as was the custom due to the hose cart's low pressure. As the *America*'s stream stopped during the changeover, the *Chicago*'s overworked piston pump suddenly ground to a halt. In that moment, the fire leaped across Taylor Street. The blaze would reach the roof of St. Paul's church and from there, fire brands would be carried on the wind and virtually all of Chicago's downtown and north side would be destroyed.

A steam pumper and its wide-eyed driver careen through a cityscape in an 1885 painting by R. A. Fox and J. A. Fraser Jr. Except for the number of horses (two instead of four), this dramatic illustration is probably not far from the truth if you imagine this to be the pumper *Little Giant* racing toward the flames that would eventually destroy Chicago. *Courtesy, CIGNA Museum and Art Collection*

MUTUAL AID
HELPING HANDS AT THE GREAT CHICAGO FIRE

The steam pumper from Aurora No. 1 that helped fight the Chicago Fire poses with the lads of that engine company in 1892. The firehouse was built in 1856, and it was from this building the pumper was dispatched, moving by rail from Aurora to the Baltimore & Ohio Railroad yard on Chicago's near west side. *Aurora Regional Fire Museum collection*

In fire department parlance, "mutual aid" means calling on neighboring fire departments for assistance in quelling a fire that has intensified beyond the capability of the local company. By the dawn of Oct. 9, 1871, there was no doubt: the great blaze engulfing Chicago was out of control. Panic had gripped the city. Every bit of useful apparatus had been committed, and the exhausted firemen were doggedly standing their ground wherever they could, but the cause was hopeless.

Telegraphers had been burning the wires since they were rousted from their beds, calling to communities surrounding the city for assistance. Doors swung open at firehouses as far north as Milwaukee, Wisconsin, and east to Cincinnati, Ohio. Off-duty railroad locomotive crews were dragged from sound sleep to get down to their rail yards and fire up available locomotives. Flatcars and boxcars were collected by yard switchers and made into trains for express trips to Chicago.

Of the many departments that responded, two companies—Elgin and Aurora, both some 40 miles west of Chicago—were typical. In the early hours of Monday, Oct. 9, 1871, the alarm reached Aurora's 1850s-era two-story firehouse. The on-duty driver made his way down from the second floor to the bay where the city's steam pumper waited. As he swung open the wood doors, the first volunteers arrived.

Meanwhile, at the nearby Chicago, Burlington & Quincy Railroad yard, a special train was being made up for the high-speed trip. To the east, the clouds were glowing orange from the distant conflagration as volunteers hand-hauled the steamer down dirt streets to a rail siding. With ropes and straining muscles, the men wheeled the engine

ABOVE: The *James T. Gifford* Silsby Third Class rotary steam pumper in front of its firehouse when it was new—and about to be sent to Chicago to help fight the Great Fire of 1871. Elgin Fire Department purchased the *Gifford* in 1869 for $8,475. *Elgin Fire Barn No. 5 Fire Museum Collection*

LEFT: The *James T. Gifford* as it appeared, gloriously restored, 128 years after its purchase by the Elgin Fire Department. It is shown outside the Elgin Fire Barn No. 5 Museum in 1997.

onto a flatcar. There were no stock cars on hand that could accommodate horses, but 85 volunteers had reported so they made do with existing railcars. With drive wheels spinning until they gripped sand sprayed on the rails, the CB&Q locomotive finally lurched forward. The emergency train roared east at full throttle, whistle screaming down a cleared right-of-way.

When the special entourage arrived, they were directed to head for Lake Michigan and put their hard suction line into the water. The Aurora men protested: They had come to fight the fire! The Chicago foreman explained that the water mains had collapsed, and several steam pumpers were forming lines from the Lake and the Chicago River—one engine pumping to the next and so on until water reached the flames. Grumbling, but game, the Aurora firefighters asked for horses. There were none. Taking turns at the ropes, the firemen hand-hauled the steamer five miles to the north where they went into line to help save the city.

They worked all day and their first rest came at 3 a.m. Tuesday morning. At 10:15 a.m., the superheated pumper burst a flue shutting off its steam. Word went out to the CB&Q in Aurora. Another special train was made up bringing steam-locomotive mechanics from the yard and a new flue. With the flue installed, the Aurora men went back to work and were finally released on Wednesday, October 11, with a commendation from the Chicago Fire Department.

The Elgin Fire Department responded to the same frantic Monday morning call when the telegraph chattered in their two-story brick fire barn on South Grove Street.

Driver Charles Morris Jennings hitched up the *James T. Gifford*, their new Silsby third-class steam pumper, and drove it down to the Chicago & North Western Railway siding and up onto a waiting flatcar. His engineer arrived, and Jennings saw to it that the two horses were boxed in and tethered in place. The locomotive put on full steam heading southeast toward the inferno. When Jennings and the Gifford arrived, they reported to Chicago's Engine 17 house from which all arriving apparatus was dispatched. The Silsby pumper and team were directed to a place on the Chicago River where they went into a line of steamers sending water toward the fighting engines and crews. There they worked in the heat and falling ash until relieved on Wednesday.

Five years later, Elgin requested the loan of a steam pumper from Chicago while the Silsby was being repaired. Chicago responded immediately, sending an engine to the town. It was returned with

thanks when the Silsby came back from the shop. A week later, Chicago sent the Elgin Fire Department a bill for the rental.

In 1887, the *Gifford* finally gave up the ghost, and Aurora loaned the town a pumper until Elgin's new water works was completed which allowed Elgin to use pressurized water mains and hose companies until 1925 when motorized fire engines were purchased.

Chris Ahrens, a German immigrant who had apprenticed under Alexander Lattam, eventually wound up as president of his own C.

Charles Morris Jennings drove the *James T. Gifford's* team at the Great Chicago Fire on October 9 and 10, 1871. *Elgin Fire Barn No. 5 Fire Museum Collection*

Ahrens & Company, manufacturing steam pumpers. On the morning of October 9, 1871, he received a visit from Miles Greenwood, Chief Engineer of the Cincinnati (Ohio) Fire Department. Greenwood explained that a great fire was burning in Chicago and asked Ahrens if there were any steam pumpers available that had not yet been delivered. Chicago Fire Chief Robert Williams had sent a telegram to Greenwood asking of any aid.

On the floor was a brand new engine ready to go to Cincinnati for display. Without hesitation, the Ahrens engine was loaded onto flatcars along with two other steamers and their crews from the Cincinnati Department.

As soon as the engines reached Chicago at 6 o'clock that evening, they were immediately put into line. Miles Greenwood had traveled with them and once the men and machines were working, he went to Engine 17's house where out-of-town help was being coordinated. He saw a tall man with a full beard wearing a white chief's hat.

"Chief Williams?" Greenwood asked. "I'm Miles Greenwood from Cincinnati."

"I've always wanted to meet you," Williams said, shaking the elder man's hand.

"I'm sorry our meeting had to be brought about by something like this," Greenwood replied as they were handed cups of coffee by one of the women who had set up a makeshift canteen near the station.

"It was bound to happen," Williams sighed. "Day after day with no rain and a high wind. We knew we were heading for a big burn."

They spoke for a while, then Williams headed toward the North Division. Greenwood finished his coffee and returned to his working machines. The Ahrens steamers pumped for 38 hours without a shutdown. Later, Chicago would buy 115 Ahrens Steam fire engines and the young immigrant would go on to hire Charles Fox. Their combined talents would eventually lead to creating the Ahrens-Fox Fire Engine Company on August 9, 1910, producing the America's finest firefighting apparatus.

Eventually, fire departments from Elgin, Aurora, and other surrounding Illinois towns and from as far away as Janesville and Milwaukee, Wisconsin, and Cincinnati, Ohio, emptied their firehouses and sent steam pumpers on railroad flat cars to help fight the blaze. Most had no horses and had to be hand-hauled to their fighting locations. Engine 17's house at 80 West Lake Street became the rallying point for out-of-town companies. Some Chicago women set up a kitchen near that house to serve the beleaguered firemen.

By the time the last home had burned at about 3 a.m. on Tuesday, October 10, the city had lost thousands of dwellings and businesses, and approximately 250 citizens had died. The Chicago Fire Department had lost eight firehouses as well as the Fire Department Store Room—destroyed in the Saturday blaze—and its headquarters housed in City Hall. No firemen were killed, but many were later hospitalized from exhaustion, smoke inhalation, and burns. No body of determined men could have done more.

A two-horse steamer, a hose cart, and a ladder truck all race to a blaze circa 1870s. At the start of the Great Chicago Fire, a steam pumper of this type would have come from the firehouse of Engine No. 6, the one-horse hose cart from the *America* Hose No. 2 station, and the ladder truck from the *Protector* (Truck No. 2) side of the *Chicago* fire house. *Courtesy, CIGNA Museum and Art Collection.*

Friendship Fire Company of Alexandria, Virginia, was founded in 1774, and its Italianate-style house, with its detailed cornices and elaborate bell tower, was built in 1855. Legend has it that George Washington was part of the original volunteer fire company. The first floor "engine room" accommodates at least three pieces of hand-hauled apparatus. Parked in front is an example of a 1770 "coffee grinder" hand pumper (see page 35).

CHAPTER 2

Firehouses From the Revolutionary War to the 1880s

A SMALL SHED, FLEET FEET, AND STRONG BACKS

Early fire fighting in eighteenth-century America was a community affair. Everyone was required to keep fire buckets in the house. When the call went out to ". . . fetch your buckets!" citizens brought them from home to form bucket brigades leading from nearest water supply to the fire. Some communities banded together a group of volunteers who would take charge at fires and direct the action. A supply of buckets was needed that was not dependent on citizen contributions in times of stress. Bill hooks for pulling down roofs, ladders, and other tools were also needed. To store the buckets and tools, towns often erected a shed.

In Mount Holly, New Jersey, the earliest known firehouse in America stands next door to the Relief Fire Engine Company No. 1, at 17 Pine Street. It is a little shed roughly eight feet wide, twelve feet long, and eight feet high with no windows. The clapboard outbuilding is the original pre-colonial home of the Britannia Fire Company, organized in 1752 when Mount Holly was then known as Bridgeton. Back then, you couldn't get into that town without crossing a bridge; you still can't.

The company roster was 13 men comprising a bucket brigade. When the alarm was sounded, they hotfooted out to this shed (originally set up in a corner of St. Andrews Grave Yard), grabbed two buckets apiece, and ran toward the smoke while shouting. Following the Revolution, the lads put their muskets back over the mantle piece and, in 1787, changed their outfit's name to the Mount Holly Fire Company. The town took a shine to that name and Bridgeton became Mount Holly, becoming the first town to be named after a fire company.

Eventually, in 1827, America's first firehouse was sold to a local farmer for $12. Somehow, the humble hut remained upright and useful for over a hundred years until a local historian discovered it in the 1950s. All the other similar storage sheds had long ago fueled the fires of America's Manifest Destiny.

Fire companies of the early nineteenth century were still casual organizations, meeting in taverns, or wherever they could find enough chairs. The very nature of their volunteer work— braving smoke and flames with water buckets and pike poles to keep the fire from leveling the town—bred a camaraderie, a mutual identity with a noble effort. That identity demanded recognition. No simple lapel pin for them, the men chose brightly colored costumes to be worn at meetings and local parades and eventually adopted uniforms to wear on the job. Usually, the parade outfit was more decorative consisting of decorated top hats, capes, and belted blouses with much leather trim such as wrist cuffs and galluses (suspenders). The working suit was more utilitarian. Red shirts were the norm together with high boots and the spreading popularity of a leather hat invented by New York fireman Henry Gratacap in 1828. It had a metal shield identifying the fire company on the front of its crown and the brim was elongated at the back to protect the fireman's neck from sparks and water. The design has lasted until the present.

Later, the speaking trumpet became another useful

Leather fire buckets were the first stage of evolution in early fire-fighting endeavors. *Courtesy Allendale Fire Museum, Allendale, Michigan.*

ABOVE: The fire-engine shed is the last building on the right at the end of the row of buildings. This modest hut is home of the Assistance Engine Hose Company where a hand-drawn hose cart was kept in 1841. *Courtesy CIGNA Museum and Art Collection.*

RIGHT: The oldest firehouse in the United States, this unassuming shed in Mount Holly, New Jersey, was built in 1798 to house ladders and buckets for the Relief Fire Company. For $12, it was carted off to become a farmer's storage shed in 1827, then a tool shed in a graveyard. Today, it is a historic one-of-a-kind building.

accessory. Amidst the chaotic swirl of action at a fire scene, the company foreman usually employed this trumpet to amplify his voice, shouting directions and egging his men on to greater effort at the pump handles and on the ladders. "Come lads! Stove in her sides! Will you pump harder boys? To the roof, men and be quick!" At moments of celebration, one end of the trumpet could be corked up and the instrument filled with a suitable beverage.

Technology took a hand to further solidify the identity of the volunteer fire fighter through the introduction of the hand-pumped fire engine. The first models were imported from England, but American industry was soon cranking out models most communities could afford. Volunteer fire departments across the post-colonial United States were eager to pony up the funds for such machines. Now, firefighters were not just bucket-tossers, they were specialists!

The earliest hand-pumped machines date from a device used on a fire in January 12, 1673, and patented as a "fire engine" in 1677 by Jan van der Heyden in Amsterdam. The early hand-pumped machines were built of wood and sprayed water on a fire from a water-cannon type nozzle attached to the machine. Buckets were used to slosh water into the machine's zinc-lined tub while volunteers furiously pumped on levered arms with wooden handles called "brakes." Single-piston pumps spritzed the water in short squirts while dual piston pumps produced a steady and effective stream. With the improvement of these fire "engines" and their increase in size and complexity, the firemen needed a bigger shed.

Meeting two needs actually set the pattern for the modern firehouse in the early nineteenth century. One need was technology and the other was ego. The stature of the volunteer firefighter had grown in American communities. What had been a community obligation—fighting fires—now centered on a select group of men who trained for the job. The names they chose for their organizations reflected the overwrought sentiment of the period, but also gave a clue to the perceived seriousness of their mission: "Good Intent," "Hand in Hand," "Relief," Respite," "Friendship," "Good Hope," "Vigilant," "Invincible," "The Ancient Rams," etc. Their slogans suggested heroic tableaux and chest-thumping proclamations: "When Help Calls, It is Our Duty to Obey," "Fearless of Danger," and "The Public Good is Our Only Aim."

While the public good was a noble mission, the boys had another agenda as well. As fire companies proliferated—often a small town might have three or

Parade outfits of Philadelphia's Hibernian Engine Company of the 1850s. The only thing firemen of the period liked better than running to a fire was marching in parades.

This beaten and etched silver speaking trumpet was designed to be used to shout orders at the fire scene, but presentation models such as this one were often left at the firehouse—sometimes to be corked at the narrow end and filled with champagne at parties. The leather hat is from the Hope Hose Company No. 5 of Philadelphia. *Courtesy Allendale Fire Museum, Allendale, Michigan.*

four volunteer companies absorbing three-quarters of the male population—town fathers bent over backwards to accommodate their needs. A sense of competition was in the air, and more fire companies meant better protection for businesses and lower insurance rates. The fire shed became the firehouse as second stories were added for additional storage space while the prized hand pumper and later hose cart occupied the main floor. By the 1850s, any town that did not have a fire company with its own firehouse was considered hopelessly backward.

Who could resist the idea of responding to the fire bell, donning on your red shirt, canvas pants, and wide-brim fire hat. Then you ran to the firehouse where you met your fellows. The doors were flung open, and shouts of "stand clear!" were raised. All the strong young men took a place at the pair of hauling ropes and out the door you ran with the pumping machine rattling behind over the cobbles and a man running in front holding a lantern high.

Even the smallest rural community was faced with a need to provide water sources for their volunteers. In those days of wood construction and storage of highly flammable horse fodder alongside kerosene for lighting, fire was a constant menace. Water cisterns, piping systems, and hydrants became town council priorities.

Parade leather belts and decorative wrist cuffs illustrate just how serious firefighters were about presenting themselves to townsfolk and competing engine companies. *Courtesy Allendale Fire Museum, Allendale, Michigan.*

Uniforms ranged from being somber attire, such as the coat from Montgomery Hose Company, to vibrant, as represented by a typical red shirt belonging to the Susquehanna Company No. 4, of Columbia, Pennsylvania. The leather helmet between them dates from the mid to late 1800s. *Courtesy Allendale Fire Museum, Allendale, Michigan.*

A scene from the Currier & Ives' series "The Life of the Fireman" shows a foreman with his speaking trumpet at a blaze where two hand-hauled engines and two ladder companies are fully engaged. Note the red shirts that symbolized volunteer companies. *Courtesy CIGNA Museum and Art Collection.*

An advertisement for the "fire engine" built by Jan van der Heyden in 1673 in Amsterdam proclaims the invention of the hand-pumped machine that also used a hose to both draft water from a well or canal and to bring it to the fire. The hose concept was lost for a while in America in lieu of the pumper-mounted water cannon of the late 1700s. *Courtesy CIGNA Museum and Art Collection.*

ABOVE: A "hay wagon" hand pumper dated 1882 with a wood platform that unfolds at the fire scene. Four or more men can stand on the platform to work the pump handles ("brakes") to throw a spritz on each down stroke. *American Museum of Firefighting Collection.*

LEFT: Closeup view of the Newsham & Ragg "coffee-grinder" hand-operated pumper that appears on the lead photo of this chapter. Built in 1770, its zinc-lined tub was filled with buckets while four men cranked and one man directed the steady water stream. *Friendship Museum Collection, Alexandria, Virginia.*

The early firehouses were utilitarian. Firefighting apparatus, whether it was a four-wheel wagon carrying buckets or a modern hand-pumper engine, was housed downstairs ready for action. Upstairs was a storage space with possibly a cot for a watchman who manned the observation tower and rang the fire bell to summon the volunteers. Some towns used watchmen who patrolled the streets carrying ratchets that they twirled, creating an annoying clatter to wake the populace when a blaze was discovered. The firehouse was, basically, where the volunteers went to get their equipment. But as the fraternalism of the fire companies became deeper rooted, the firehouse became a social center. The stairs to the second floor became off-limits for the general public. Admittance was by fire company members only.

In 1817, two Philadelphia firemen, James Sellers and Abraham Pennock, patented an improved leather hose that was riveted for strength. Sewn leather hose had been available, but its failure rate made companies hang onto their deck nozzles. Sellers and Pennock's hose specifications were:

Hibernia Engine Company No. 1 in Philadelphia, Pennsylvania, was the very model of a modern volunteer fire company in 1857. Togged out in their best with their decorated hand-pumper fire engine in front of their own building, these were men to be admired—and a club to be joined, if possible. *Courtesy CIGNA Museum and Art Collection.*

HIBERNIA FIRE ENGINE COMPANY. N.º 1.
OF PHILADELPHIA.

"Pure oak, city tanned, Baltimore, or Philadelphia leather, known as 'overweight,' the average weight not less than 22 pounds to the side, none less than 20 pounds, double riveted with copper wire, size known as No. 8, 22 rivets to the running foot; splices made with 13 rivets of a size known as No. 7 wire, finished with three loops and rings and weight no less than 64 pounds to each 50 feet, exclusive of couplings and warranted to stand a pressure of not less than 200 pounds to the square inch."

Interestingly, Boston firemen in the 1820s considered the use of hose to be cowardly. They preferred to maneuver their hand pumper as close as possible to the flames and use the water cannon nozzle mounted on the tub. "The nearer the fire, the higher the post of honor," they proclaimed.

The addition of hose reels to the volunteers' fire-fighting arsenal swelled the need for new members. All of the fire-fighting apparatus had to be hand-hauled to the fire. The Friendship Company's pumper and hose cart needed fleet-footed runners on the tow ropes to get to the blaze. They needed hose men to find a hydrant or cistern water supply and hook up both suction and output lines. Facing the flames, strong backs bent to the brakes, heaving some 60 strokes a minute, up-down, up-down. As the water sprayed, a volunteer ladder company would arrive and rush their ladders into position to rescue, or do meaningful work with their pike poles and axes to ventilate the building.

The proliferation of volunteer companies covering overlapping areas of a city generated a competition between them to be ". . . the first in." This competition required the addition of specialized members, strong boys, hard of eye and fast of fist. Often, a single hydrant would be nearest a fire scene. The company runners literally raced any other company responding to the same alarm. Whoever got to the fire plug first had the "place of honor" nearest the flames with their stream. The hired muscle boys were sent racing ahead of the fire-fighting apparatus to secure the plug and whack the dickens out of any other late arrivals who might want to

"Start her lively, boys," shouts the fore-man to his mates as they answer a night call in this Currier & Ives print of an 1854 firehouse and engine company. *Courtesy CIGNA Museum and Art Collection.*

ABOVE:These devices were among the earliest fire alarms. In 1648, city officials of New Amsterdam, New York, appointed eight volunteers to form a "rattle watch." The rattle (left) was twirled to create a racket when a fire was spotted. The alarm would then be taken up by church bells to rouse the volunteers. The muffin bell (right) was an improvement on the rattle. *Courtesy Allendale Fire Museum, Allendale, Michigan.*

RIGHT: Bucket machines—this one dates from about 1840—were used in outlying communities where no hydrants existed. Buckets were filled from wells and cisterns. Run by the Continental Bucket Company No. 1 of Jamaica, New York, between 1860 and 1890, this vehicle is considered a "racer" and shows marks of upsets and collisions. *American Museum of Firefighting Collection.*

stick their hoses in. These boys were called "plug-uglies." These hulking worthies were the fore-runners of things to come. The opening lines of a song written for the Ancient Rams Fire Company No. 2 of Southwark in Philadelphia around the 1850's gives us a hint of their priorities.

We are the Ancient Rams,
Who never fear our foes,
At the corner of Second and Wharton we stand
And run with the WECCA Hose.

Then arouse ye gallant Rams,
And by the WECCA stand,
And show unto our friends and foes
That we're a sporting band.

DES & LITH. BY JONAS.

PUBLISHED & PRINTED BY PRIFF.

THE WHITE TURTLE, & THE RED CRAB

RESPECTFULLY DEDICATED TO THE NORTHERN LIBERTY HOSE Co.

The song goes on to describe the Rams as "boys of fun and glee" who "drive dull care away" by pounding to a pulp any competing fire company met on the fire ground. A noble sentiment, but hardly reassuring to the local insurance brokers.

All across the country, volunteer companies sprouted. Town councils were very happy with the rush to good citizenship and helped each fledgling department grow. The volunteer firemen were lionized. Currier & Ives produced melodramatic series of prints based on the firefighter's heroism. Songs and poems were penned, some hopelessly mawkish in their sentimentality. A few, however came from more inspired hands. In 1855, Walt Whitman wrote of an injured fireman, a step down from the Paul Bunyan status of most heroes of the time.

I am the mash'd fireman with breastbone broken,
Tumbling walls buried me in their debris,
Heat and smoke I inspired, I heard the yelling
*   shouts of my comrades,*
I heard the distant pick of their picks and shovels,
They have cleared the beams away, they tenderly
*   lift me forth.*

I lie in the night air in my red shirt, the pervad-
*   ing hush is for my sake,*
Painless after all I lie exhausted, but not unhappy,
White and beautiful are the faces around me, the
*   heads are bared of their firecaps,*
The kneeling crowd fades with the light of the
*   torches.*

The "White Turtle" and the "Red Crab" race toward a fire for the privilege of being "the first one in." These two hose wagons have bells clanging as dogs and pedestrians flee. A tie at the fire plug could mean an all out donnybrook of flying fists and paving stones. Note the informal outfits of these boys, suggesting a nighttime call. *Courtesy CIGNA Museum and Art Collection.*

continued on page 43

Nothing stirs the hearts and souls of a country's citizens quite as much as a rousing patriotic anthem. Colonists followed the revolutionary banner inspired by such songs as "Yankee Doodle" and "God Save America;" during the nineteenth century, Americans were inspired by "Dixie," "Rally 'Round the Flag, Boys," and "Battle Hymn of the Republic."

Loyalty, fierce competition, and jealousy were especially strong among the firefighting companies in mid-nineteenth century Philadelphia. This led to inspirational verse and music composed by volunteer members,

"The Man With the Ladder and the Hose." This illustrated song was a standard form of entertainment in movie houses and dance halls from the 1890's to 1911. Its popularity faded with the coming of the player piano and improved technology in phonographs. Then, as feature films became longer, the illustrated song outlasted its usefulness and passed into history. While in its heyday, the "illustrations" provided work for many rising film stars.

probably to keep the competitive spirits flowing. The following excerpts from the "Franklin Hose Song" (written in the latter part of the eighteenth century), starts out with an account of a false alarm apparently sent to Philadelphia's Franklin Hose Company by the rival Good Will Company on Christmas night. Upon their return, the men of the Franklin were "attacked by thousands of bloodhounds" whom they fought "with manly resistance . . . until we were forced away." Unwilling to take this humiliation lying down, they lost no time in seeking retaliation:

Early next morning,
We all resolved to stand,
While vengeance beat in every breast,
From a boy up to a man

The alarm of Fire being given
Onward we did go
Their house we broke, and their Engine took,
And beat their members also
Unfortunately, they were apprehended and arraigned:
Grames and McReynolds plead guilty
And got nine months a-piece
We then petitioned the governor
To get their release.

Clemency was denied. In the following verse, a gentleman known as John Burns was forced to spend the next three years in jail, although the song neglected to mention the reason for such severe punishment. The cause for the original "bloodhound attack" appears to be political:

Bad luck attend that man;
And silenced be his tongue
Who swore we cheered for Britain,
And cursed our Washington!

The Good Will Company, not to be outdone, drew on the talent of their creative members who composed the "Good Will Hose Song," its primary theme being the lambasting of another group known as The Bleeders. Following are some of the more stirring verses:

The "Bleeders" of fighting so often have boasted,
But still when we meet them they never will stand,
For if they would do so, they'd surely get roasted
For they are but boys, and a cowardly band.
They have to depend on their friends for to back them;
Surrounded by friends they're in dread of us still,
We never yet have been afraid to attack them,
for cowards have never run with the Good Will.

If the word "weenie" had been part of the lexicon of that period, it most likely would have found its way into the second stanza which only reiterated the sentiments of the first:

......They dread the Tormentors, and always will fear them
For we have been ever their bitterest pill,
They tremble like cowards whenever we're near them
A Bleeder will start at the name of Good Will.

And if that weren't enough, "The Bleeders" were dullards, lacking in originality:

They think with their song they have cut a big figure
They think it so clever because it is long,
...Of all we have seen, 'tis the silliest song,

If the "Bleeders" were as warlike as any of the other volunteer companies of the time, they most likely took up the challenge of the final verse:

Then let them attack us whenever they're willing,
They'll find that we fear not a parcel of boys,
And then we shall see who will do the most killing
And also who's able to make the most noise.

By the 1840s and 1850s, volunteer fire companies developed into tight-knit social clubs, and as time went on, their get-togethers became more and more elaborate. Although rivalry continued, the public had grown weary of their aggressive behavior. More civilized forms of entertainment were festive dinners, dances, and receptions. Firefighters always found a place on their social calendars for any venue that offered the chance to perform or engage in a rousing sing-a-long, extolling the firefighter's heroics. The New York City Fire Department had 60 companies and each held at least one ball every winter. These events were instituted as money-raising endeavors, to purchase uniforms and equipment for the volunteers, and everyone in the community was invited to participate. In 1877 the Providence, Rhode Island, Fire Department offered a variety of dance music; guests swayed to such melodies as "304 Alarms Last Year" and the "Every Man With An Axe" waltz.

Award ceremonies, as well, began and ended with stirring melodies lauding the unselfish dedication of the gallant fireman. One song even commemorated the retired fire man:

The Veteran Firemen's Song

What though our hair is gray
The old "machine's" our idol
We love to see her play
And squirt her waters tidal

About the same time, musicals in the home became a popular means of entertainment. In households across the country, the piano was regarded with the same reverence as TV sets are today. Songs on sheet music relayed such sentiments as affection, domestic bliss, and high moral standards.

Professional entertainment grew in popularity during the latter nineteenth and early twentieth centuries. Music halls, dime museums, vaudeville, and silent movies offered pleasant diversions from the pianolas found in America's parlors. One medium was the "illustrated song" used as a filler between live acts in theaters or as film reels were changed in silent-movie houses. The soloist sang while his slides were projected on the screen, and, so that the audience could sing along, the chorus lyrics were flashed at various points in the program. One of these "song plays," called "The Man With The Ladder And The Hose," praised the gallant fireman as he answered a midnight call to save a mother and her two

An early, rather melodramatic lantern slide used (usually in a theater house) to illustrate the song "The Main With the Ladder and the Hose." A mother, putting her children to bed, sees a fire in the next-door building. She and the children are eventually rescued by a gallant fireman. *Courtesy CIGNA Museum and Art Collection.*

children. Joe Maxwell and Al Simpson, a popular vaudeville team of the period, delighted fire chiefs, commissioners, and other fire-department members with this "illustrated song" paying tribute to their heroics.

By the early 1920s as entertainment became more sophisticated, people used their leisure time for movies, knocking on the doors of "speakeasies" and going for rides in their Ford Flivvers. Firemen became less competitive as paid departments replaced the volunteer companies, and the firefighter became a civil servant. City planners and managers sought to transform the image and structure of their fire departments from the parade-marching sentiments prevalent in the nineteenth century to a technically-specialized industry. The firefighter still socialized with his fellow workers, but this might be limited to the occasional dinner dance or getting together at each other's homes. However, their creativity in capturing the spirit of the heroic and sometimes violent aspects of these early days has been preserved in these lusty and sentimental lyrics that one can imagine booming forth from a shoulder-to-shoulder gathering of well-lubricated throats.

(Courtesy CIGNA Museum and Art Collection. Music by T. Mayo Geary; copyright 1904 by The American Advance Music Co., New York, New York)

FRIENDSHIP FIRE COMPANY, ALEXANDRIA, VIRGINIA

The Friendship Fire Company was the first volunteer fire company organized in Alexandria in 1774. It was a time when fire prevention was on prosperous merchants' minds. Benjamin Franklin, up in Philadelphia, founded the first volunteer fire company in 1736 and also established the first fire insurance company called "Hand-In-Hand." Legend has it that George Washington was an active volunteer firefighter and a member of the Friendship Company, though there isn't a scrap of paper to prove it. Oral tradition has been honored, and his connection with the company has been accepted. He did not live to see the current home of the company that was built on South Alfred Street in 1855.

Its design reflects the colonial heritage of Alexandria complete with a white cupola watchtower stuck on top. Inside, the restoration has been excellent, recreating the second-floor meeting room with some original furniture. The lads of the Friendship Fire Company met up there to plan the activities of their club and to elect new members. The election process they used was common among firehouses at the time and continued with volunteer groups through to the mid-twentieth century. A two-compartment box was placed on the table. One compartment held a mixture of white and black marbles, and the other was empty, covered by a lid with a small opening on the end. One by one, members would file up to the box, choose a marble and push it into the opening. When all had voted. The other end of the box was opened and if there were more than an agreed-upon number of black marbles in the mix, the member was refused entry. He had been, as is still said, "black-balled." Such a rejection could be ruinous in a small community. If the fellow was accepted by the company, the local calligrapher was put to work to fill in the appropriate blanks on the company's incredibly ornate membership certificate, suitable for framing.

The Friendship Firehouse was probably built to house the magnificent "Philadelphia-style" hand-pump engine purchased four years earlier, in 1851. This style of pumper had its pumping arms ("brakes") located at the ends of the machine. They unfolded and locked into place. Twenty-two men working in two shifts were required to work the brakes and keep up a steady stream until the fire was put out, or everyone fainted.

Displayed on the downstairs engine-room floor, this machine is a good example of the money and pride lavished by the membership on their equipment. An improvement on the eighteenth-century tub pumper that required a bucket-brigade, this particular machine was adapted to use hose and draft from a hydrant, a well, or a pond. In 1858, the Friendship Company added a hose reel carriage to their roster that is also on display.

As the twentieth century opened, architects found themselves faced with a variety of challenges depending on the depth of their clients' pockets. For example, in Maryland around 1853, the Independent Fire Company of Baltimore was riding a peak of popularity. To solidify their identity and memorialize their fire company's name, architects Reasin and Wetherald were hired to take the idea of a watch-tower/bell tower/hose-hanging tower and run with it. They produced a top-heavy, 117-foot "sky-scraper" modeled after Giotto's Campanile in Florence, Italy. The house served the hand pumper company as they kept watch over the part of town called "Old Baltimore." In 1859, the City took over the building, and it became Engine Company 6 when the department switched to steam. In 1880, a four-faced clock was added just above the huge bell chamber. In the early 1990s the house was closed

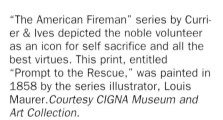

"The American Fireman" series by Currier & Ives depicted the noble volunteer as an icon for self sacrifice and all the best virtues. This print, entitled "Prompt to the Rescue," was painted in 1858 by the series illustrator, Louis Maurer. *Courtesy CIGNA Museum and Art Collection.*

The Resolution Hose & Steam Fire Engine Company of Philadelphia was very effusive in its acceptance certificates. The new member must have felt like he had received a knighthood. In volunteer firemen circles, it must be remembered, every fire call was a re-affirmation of membership in the face of possible death. *Courtesy CIGNA Museum and Art Collection.*

A painting of Benjamin Franklin completed after his death in 1790 depicting him as a young volunteer fireman. He founded the first company in America in 1736, but never wore the style of helmet shown on his head. This fire helmet was invented in 1836 by Henry Gratacap of New York City. Looking closely, you can see it sits slightly askew on his head since it was probably added to the painting later. *Courtesy CIGNA Museum and Art Collection.*

This "Philadelphia-style" hand pumper was purchased by the Friendship Company in 1851. The pumping arms, or "brakes," are located at the ends of the machine and could be unfolded to allow the 20 men who pulled it to the fire to pump the water. *Friendship Museum Collection, Alexandria, Virginia.*

A hand-drawn hose-reel carriage in the Friendship Museum Collection, Allendale, Michigan. Colorfully painted and built for speed, the carriage reel contained 400 to 600 feet of leather hose. *Friendship Museum Collection, Alexandria, Virginia.*

Originally the Independent Fire Company of Baltimore, Maryland, then Engine No. 6 and now a fire museum, this firehouse with its Italianate-style tower was designed in 1853 by architects Reasin and Wetherald. The facility was closed as a firehouse in 1976. *Ron Mattes Collection.*

and converted into a fire museum. When it closed, it was the oldest active firehouse in the U.S.

FIREHOUSE NO. 1, GALENA, ILLINOIS

At the other end of the architectural scale is Firehouse No. 1 in Gen. Ulysses S. Grant's home town of Galena in northwestern Illinois; this firehouse was built in 1852 and is believed to be the oldest in the state. Parked in front of the building is its original tenant, a very rare Agnew pumper built in Philadelphia with pump brakes at the ends, a copy of the German Shanghai machine mechanism. The "Old Musheen," as it was nicknamed, can use either fire buckets or a suction hose to fill its tub. The "Musheen" arrived in Galena in 1855 after the city shelled out $1,600, and it served for over 50 years.

Although built in the Italianate style with overhung roof, corbels and the watchtower, it is a structure without frills— a no-nonsense red brick building that replaced a smaller brick structure built on the same ground that was used to store fire buckets and tools. The firehouse was the first of six houses built to protect this important lead-mining town that was expected to rival Chicago. Called Liberty Fire Company No. 1, it represented a reorganization of two companies organized in 1836, the Cataract Fire Engine Company No. 1 and the Neptune Fire Company No. 2.

In the process of restoration inside and out—it suffers from rising dampness and lingering mounds of bat guano—when it was in full-time operation, Galena's Firehouse No. 1 was home for a sturdy breed of volunteers, considering the steep hills down to any fire in the town center and the returning climb back to quarters.

VOLUNTEERS FLAUNT THEIR MUSCLE AND HAVE A BALL

With the number of fire companies growing and memberships swelling, volunteer firemen organized into tight-knit groups becoming important tools for political parties and individuals. In cities and large towns, politicians competed for the volunteer firemen's support just like today's candidates court organized labor unions. Contributions to firemen's retirement funds and financial help with building and outfitting new firehouses became a way of political life.

The firehouse, meanwhile, had grown into something considerably more than a convenient storage space. While serious money was lavished on decorat-

The Galena, Illinois, firehouse built in 1852 to serve the "Liberty Fire Company No. 1." Thought to be the oldest firehouse in Illinois, this two-story building features the Italianate roof overhangs and corbels typical of the period. Sighted on a hill over-looking downtown Galena, one of the state's most well-known tourist magnets, the building's tower housed a fire bell to summon volunteers. Parked in front is the "Old Musheen," an Agnew hand pumper bought in 1855.

ABOVE: Dressed in their parade best, volunteers of the Galena Liberty Fire Company No. 1 stand by their hose reel with the Old Musheen hand pumper in the rear during the Civil War era. *Galena/Jo Daviess County Historical Society & Museum Collection.*

ing equipment, even more went into the interior furnishings and the glittering sideboards awaiting guests at evening entertainments. The firehouse became the place to party. According to one English visitor to one of New York City's central firehouses in 1857:

> "...the walls were hung with portraits of Washington, Franklin, Jefferson, Mason, and other founders of the Republic; the floor was covered with velvet-pile carpeting, a noble chandelier hung from the centre, the crimson curtains were rich and heavy, while the sideboard was spread with claret jugs, and pieces of plate presented by citizens whose houses and property had been preserved from fire by the exertions of the brigade, or by the fire companies of other cities in testimony of their admiration for some particular act of gallantry or heroism which the newspapers had recorded."

Arrival of a new piece of equipment at the firehouse was also reason to spread out the welcome mat, pass the cigars, and have a dance.

> "The party was a glittering success, and although a very formal affair, it had all the charm of a neighborhood get-together. As one fireman put it, 'You could walk up and ask almost any lady to dance without introduction.' Sweeping gowns and sparkling jewelry bedecked the lovely ladies, and their firemen escorts danced them handsomely around the hall to gay waltzes, polkas, and quadrilles from nine o'clock until three in the morning. An occasional pause to 'sit this one out' meant a trip downstairs for a cup of punch and another stroll around the machine."

An inventory of the Hibernia Fire Engine Company firehouse dating from the hand-pumper days records some 145 line items, among them:

2 large guilt frame mirrors
1 ball banner
3 officer's chairs
1 lounge-engineer's room
2 hair-cloth sofas
15 arm chairs
1 set of officer's desks
20 white stone spittoons
6 gutta-percha spittoons
12 settees
1 marble top center table
115 yards, Brussels carpet
5 silver and plated fire horns
1 worked satin banner
1 worked velvet banner
4 coal stoves
1 gas-lit stove and pipe
2 round center tables
110 yards cocoa matting
6 parade axes
6 parade torches
6 brass lamps
1 lot funeral hat badges
1 Engine Mourning drape
40 paintings and photos in gilt and walnut frames
1 dog

Interestingly, nowhere in the entire inventory was the fire engine mentioned.

The practice of "visiting" became a common recreation for volunteer fire companies. The whole house would pack up their apparatus and head for another

LEFT: A grand parade of firemen in New York City shows the display of polished equipment, satin banners, and the companies wearing their marching best. These parades drew large crowds to see the stalwart men of the volunteer companies who were responsible for keeping the city safe. *Courtesy CIGNA Museum and Art Collection.*

LEFT: A certificate of membership for the Good Hope Hose & Steam Fire Company of Philadelphia. The graphics surrounding the text show various aspects of the life of the fireman along with the Hope Company firehouse; the reason for including the drawing of the *Ariel* sailing vessel is uncertain. *Courtesy CIGNA Museum and Art Collection.*

FACING PAGE: St. Florian, the Polish patron saint of fire protection, is depicted here on a fire-engine panel, but frequently appeared on membership certificates, sharing space with nymphs and contemporary firefighters. A room in a seventeenth century farm house in Upper Bavaria is painted with several images of the saints, including Saint Florian who is shown extinguishing a burning building. Florian is buried in an area that encompasses a seventeenth-century abbey and a fire-fighting museum. *Courtesy CIGNA Museum and Art Collection.*

During the nineteenth century, Americans imitated their European cousins in many social customs including the practice of leaving calling cards and written formal invitations. Although the calling cards were only made of pasteboard, they carried with them the weighty representations of character, surname influence, and helped to broadcast one's social position to the neighborhood. Middle-class women with ambitions toward joining the circle of those who held higher social position would present their cards when "calling on" a lady whose friendship or patronage they desired.

While the firefighters of this era didn't call upon each other and leave flowery violet-scented cards, they nevertheless were swept up in the Victorian sentiments of the period. In sharp contrast to their testosterone-laden activities such as battling rival companies for use of a fire plug or contesting to see whose hose shot the longest stream, they lavishly spared no expense on their own printed declaration of upwardly mobile social climbing—the certificate of membership.

As early as the 1700s, volunteer fire-fighting companies spent considerable time meeting, planning festivities, or just using the fire house as a place for camaraderie, not unlike their old haunts at the local taverns. Small wonder, then, that men in the community lusted after membership in the local fire companies. After undergoing strenuous examination if they were not found wanting by their peers and won a majority vote, they were admitted to the hearty circle. Once they achieved this exalted station, they were awarded an appropriately embellished membership certificate (suitable for framing).

Each organization, apparently adopting the "less is a bore" philosophy, designed its own document, sparing nothing when it came to elaborate artwork and calligraphic lettering. One of the best examples of these certificates is the one designed in 1856 for the Hope Hose Fire Company of Philadelphia, Pennsylvania. Besides the usual illustration of the company's firehouse and equipment, borders on many of the documents showed Florian, the Polish patron saint of Fire, inspiring the firemen to noble deeds. The firemen also seemed to appreciate any drawings of partially-clad goddesses and nymphs wearing filmy garments strategically-placed across their bodies, to avoid any accusations of obscenity.

Firemen's off-duty festivities evolved in sophistication as the decades progressed. From the second half of the nineteenth century to World War I, elaborate visits between fire companies occurred regularly. First, a fire company was sent an invitation to share a weekend with its counterparts in a nearby town. After accepting the invitation, the guest company feverishly began preparations for the big event. They scrubbed and waxed their most prized engine, had their uniforms cleaned and buttons polished, and finally gathered at the firehouse for a gala parade (complete with brass band and satin banners) to the railroad station or boat dock. While the firefighters boarded their transport, the fire-fighting equipment would be carefully loaded onto its flatcar or special berth and off they'd go.

Upon their arrival, the firefighters checked into the finest hotel in town—compliments of their hosts. The next several days were spent in merriment and good fellowship—each company in the visiting town provided some form of entertainment with dinners, receptions, and parades. The *spiritus frumenti* flowed freely and toasts to each other were initiated at the slightest provocation.

Of course, no visit was complete without some friendly competition. At some point during the visit, the hosts sponsored a contest, or "muster," to see which engine could pump the highest stream or who could lay a line of hose the fastest. The winning company received an ornate trophy for its efforts. Other mementos such as silver speaking

trumpets, punch bowls, and commemorative prints were exchanged. On the last day, yet another parade, accompanied again by a booming and crashing brass band, escorted the firefighters back to their transport for their return trip home.

Although the firefighters were aggressive in their on-the-job behavior, they didn't seem to lack in social refinement when they were entertained by other companies. Upon their return from the festivities, the thank-you card—that symbol of Victorian graciousness and urbanity—was sent to their hosts. Here the term "thank-you card" took on an entirely new meaning. Not satisfied with a simple note on pasteboard, many fire companies engaged the services of a local artisan to create a grandiose certificate, embellished with gold and filigree, expressing boundless gratitude for such a delightful visit to their fair city. The certificate could be as large as 24 x 40 inches, surrounded by a brass frame decorated with firemen's hats, axes, ladders, and other tools of the trade. Firemen showed equal gratitude to businesses and individuals who helped during a major fire. The card of thanks sent by the Fairmount Steam Fire Engine Co. of Philadelphia in September 1863 to the Union & Cooper Shop Volunteer Refreshment Saloons expressed their appreciation for:

> . . . the bounteous supply of Refreshments and the kindness manifested towards the Company, whilst at the fire which occurred at the U.S. Navy Yard, on the morning of the 13th inst.

By the early 1920s, most city fire companies had evolved into paid departments and rural volunteers had cleaned up their act. Fire fighting was recognized as a skilled profession, not an excuse to organize a boisterous, two-fisted club with social perquisites who also fought fires. Our way of life in America was changing. People had limited time and resources to spend on festivities lasting several days and printing up the prescribed artistry that accompanied

LEFT: A silver trophy presented to the Association of Exempt Firemen of Paterson, New Jersey, by the Liberty Fire Company No. 5 of Reading, Pennsylvania. The trophy is decorated with the symbols of fire fighting: ladder, lantern, work hat, ax, speaking trumpet, bucket, rope, and a hose with nozzle. Horse heads are on either side of the base. On the panel between the heads is an engraving of a horse-drawn steamer heading to a fire. Other than the word "Victory" on the top of the trophy, nothing indicates the reason for winning this impressive award. Perhaps the New Jersey firemen came in first in a hose-laying competition. *Courtesy CIGNA Museum and Art Collection.*

them. Since firefighters' attitudes had shifted gears and the elegantly furnished meeting rooms were now partitioned into dormitories and offices, there was limited space for social pursuits or the display of elegant trophies. When volunteer companies were supplanted by paid forces, the departing lads usually took their silver plate, framed artwork, and satin banners with them. Fortunately, many of these ornate expressions of firemen's sentiments from that breast-beating, overwrought, and quaintly delightful bygone era are still preserved today in museums across the country.

ABOVE: A "card" of thanks from a business to the Friendship Engine Company, ". . . for their ardent, energetic, generous and successful exertions in saving our property . . ." The frame is made of decorative plaster, designed by James S. Earle. Flames are shooting out of the windows at the center top of the frame. Two miniature firemen stand at each of the top corners, one speaking into his trumpet, the other handling the hose, which is attached to the pumper located at the bottom center of the frame. On the lower left corner, a firemen is ascending a ladder while carrying a hose attached to a hydrant. Scrolls adorn the top line of the roof and a cartouche with a fire hydrant in the center gives a Rococo-like finish to the bottom half. *Courtesy CIGNA Museum and Art Collection.*

firehouse in another city. There would be banquets in the upstairs meeting room and at grand hotels. Parades of polished apparatus and costumed fire fighters would file down main streets, behind spirited musical bands, awash in color and spruced-up brasswork. Ranks of satin banners proclaiming each fire and hose company rippled in the breeze. An 1820 Philadelphia parade observer noted the following splendid procession.

> "Every decoration which painters, sculptors, and labidaries [sic] could put upon them was used. They were resplendent with gold and silver work, handsome paintings, mirrored sides, and carvings. They were inlaid with pearl and one carriage bore on its front a blazing glory

formed by imitation brilliants of the first order. The very handsome machines thus decorated seemed only designed for show, while the (actual) work was done by uncouth, badly shaped, clumsy carriages called 'crabs' which bore as much resemblance to the dandy hose carriages as orang-outangs [sic] do to Venus."

A "muster" might follow which allowed the visitors to compete with the hosts to see who could lay hose the fastest or shoot water streams the highest. Upon return, elaborate thank-you gifts and cards were sent by the visiting house to the hosts and the cycle would continue. These visits strengthened the bonds between volunteer houses, so when local issues arose, national support might be requested. That time would be coming as the over-manned, over-rich, over-fed vol-

ABOVE: A very rare parade hose carriage designed by the Edward B. Leverich Company of Brooklyn, New York, sometime in the 1870s. Trimmed with gold leaf and crystal lanterns, this surviving high-wheel hose carrier must have been kept well clear of any serious fire scene. *Courtesy Allendale Fire Museum, Allendale, Michigan.*

LEFT: Close-up of oil-painted panel on the center air chamber of a double-decker hand pumper. Painted by Joseph H. Johnson, who was one of the better known "fire engine artists" prior to 1860. This is one of eight paintings on this pumper. *American Museum of Firefighting Collection.*

unteers would find themselves over-matched.

As the country headed toward the end of the 1850s, many communities began to tire of the volunteers' antics and arrogance. For all the mobs of sharply dressed firemen and for all the polished brass and oil-painted panels on the apparatus, fires were not being put out or contained. At fires, many companies employed a steward who carried a cask of brandy or other spirits to "fortify" the warriors as they toiled. Some volunteers became so fortified they couldn't stand let alone point a hose. Local establishments that purveyed such restoratives sometimes vied

with each other to keep the firemen well lubricated. Firehouses became hangouts for local toughs as the plug-uglies invited over friends. Drunken loafers passed time on the firehouse ramp making crude remarks to the proper ladies passing by. Bands of volunteer firemen penned "death threats" to rivals of the political machine.

The world had moved along. With all their romantic posturing and mawkish slogans, many of the volunteers had grown beyond being good citizens into fraternal, self-aggrandizing clubmen who looked forward to a good brawl with a rival fire company

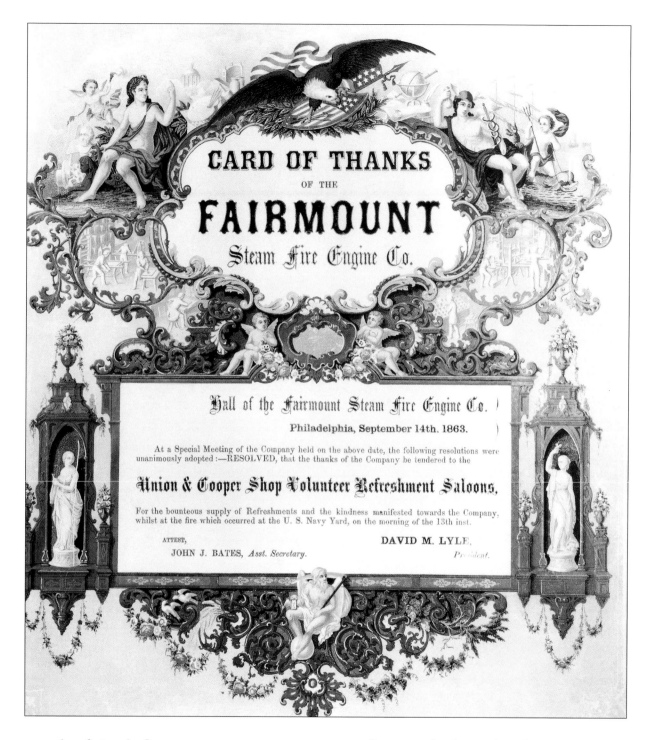

CARD OF THANKS

OF THE

FAIRMOUNT

Steam Fire Engine Co.

Hall of the Fairmount Steam Fire Engine Co.

Philadelphia, September 14th, 1863.

At a Special Meeting of the Company held on the above date, the following resolutions were unanimously adopted :—RESOLVED, that the thanks of the Company be tendered to the

Union & Cooper Shop Volunteer Refreshment Saloons,

For the bounteous supply of Refreshments and the kindness manifested towards the Company, whilst at the fire which occurred at the U. S. Navy Yard, on the morning of the 13th inst.

ATTEST,
JOHN J. BATES, *Asst. Secretary.*

DAVID M. LYLE,
President.

Here is a framed and embellished thank-you to Union & Cooper Shop Volunteer Refreshment Saloons (a chain, perhaps?) from the From the Fairmount Steam Fire Engine Company the day after providing a, ". . . bounteous supply of refreshments . . . whilst at the fire which occurred at the U. S. Navy Yard on the morning of the 13th . . ." *Courtesy CIGNA Museum and Art Collection.*

more than facing the flames.

In Cincinnati, Ohio, two inventors, Abel Shawk and Alexander Bonner Latta, were commissioned to cobble together a moveable steam-powered pump for fire-fighting. They came up with a 22,000-pound monster with all the mobility of steering a cruise ship down a trout stream. Its firehouse had a high ceiling to accommodate the tall stack and needed plenty of engine-room floor space for the number of hose carts it could service at the fire scene. At its public trial held on New Year's Day 1853, the three-wheeled, self-powered behemoth was matched with the best of the volunteer companies. When the water settled, the Shawk-Latta pumper had delivered six simultaneous streams while the volunteers lay faint on the ground from heaving on the levers. Steam was nothing new to fire-fighting by

This Shawk & Latta three-wheeled steam pumper is hauled by four straining horses down a street in Cincinnati, Ohio; this is a lighter modification of the original behemoth. A hose cart follows, towing what might be a coal wagon. The engine could maintain two streams reaching 200 feet. *Courtesy CIGNA Museum and Art Collection.*

that time. A steam pumper in New York City had shot a steam of water over a 166-foot flag pole.

Some volunteers reacted with predictable action to the invasion of steam onto their outmoded turf. They tried sabotage, beatings, and false alarms and rigged competitions to discredit the new steam rigs. "They" does not mean every volunteer. In some cases, volunteers turned over their houses to the community, sold their hand pumpers to help buy steam equipment, and put in their requests to join the city department. But in most cases, they stripped their meeting rooms down to the wood floors, carried off anything shiny, and stomped away in a huff.

As other cities saw how railway locomotive design-

ers had controlled the pressures of steam for day-to-day travel and the hauling of freight, the fear of detonating a steam bomb and taking out most of Main Street ebbed away. Trials showed the consistency of steam, its tireless output, and the need for fewer men would allow a fulltime paid force under city control. Another benefit of steam power was speed in getting the "wet stuff to the red stuff" via two, three, and four horsepower instead of beating feet on the bricks. But, horses were anathema to the runners who hand-hauled the firefighting hardware. Back in 1832 when a hook-and-ladder company was felled by a cholera epidemic, the survivors used a horse to tow the ladder wagon to the a scene. Later, some members of a

rival company sneaked into the ladder truck's firehouse, shaved the horse's mane, and painted a skunk stripe down its back.

In March 1853, Cincinnati made a landmark move by hiring the country's first part-time paid professional city fire department. The sponsors of the steam machine said of their canny purchase that was quietly percolating in a corner of the huge fire barn, "It never gets drunk. It never throws brick bats, and the only drawback connected with it is it can't vote."

The first annual report of the chief engineer, Miles Greenwood, of the Cincinnati Fire Department in 1854 backs up the city's feelings after the change-over to professional fire fighters. "Under the present con-

trol, the engine houses are no longer nurseries where the youth of the city are trained in vice, vulgarity, and debauchery, and where licentiousness holds his nightly revels. The Sabbath Day is no longer desecrated by yells and fierce conflicts of rival fire companies, who sought the occasion offered by false alarms, often gotten up for making brutal assaults on upon each other; our citizens, male and female, pass our Engine Houses without being insulted by the coarse vulgarities of the persons collected around them."

"Steam and Muscle" is the title of this Currier & Ives print showing a side-by-side trial of steam pumpers against hand-pumped engines on a fire ground. The steamers invariably won, unless sabotaged by the disgruntled volunteers. This innovation marked the beginning of the end for the volunteer departments in large cities. *Courtesy CIGNA Museum and Art Collection.*

Union Fire Company No.1 in Carlisle, Pennsylvania, was built in 1869 and is a typical example of "industrial" architecture of the period. The house uses cut stone, terra-cotta, and pre-stamped brick as decoration across its facade and tower for a three-dimension effect topped by a wood cupola and bell. These design touches announced the coming trend of Victorian mixing of textures and materials that would achieve full flower in the 1880s through the turn of the century.

CHAPTER 3
Technology Breakthroughs: 1880 to the 1900s

THE STEAM-ENGINE FIREHOUSE—SLEEPING WITH HORSES

That awesome steam power that had impressed the crowds at the Cincinnati pumper trials had been distilled down into the size of the graceful Silsby, the Amoskeag, and the La France pumpers. Ladder trucks could carry more ladders and reach higher to fight fires in the new "skyscrapers" being built in Chicago and New York.

Now, everything didn't just collapse at once. Over the years, since the original steam pumpers broke onto the fire-fighting scene, their weight had been brought down to under 8,000 pounds. The red-shirted volunteers still got their backs up over the horse issue. First, they thought the use of horses threatened their manhood. Many volunteer houses opted to hand-haul the steam pumpers just as they had done with their wooden hand pumpers rather than capitulate to the nags. One or two very busy downhill pulls in front of a four-ton, free-rolling, smoke-belching steamer full of scalding hot water showed the boys just how fast they could really run. The thought of getting the cast-iron brute back up that hill brought tears to the survivors' eyes.

Second, the idea of bunking down with horses and all the eye-watering, nose-offending side effects that went with that deal disturbed the sensibilities of many volunteers who had memories of more elegant, genteel days. As a temporary peace offering, volunteer companies were allowed to rent horses from nearby stables and farmers. When the fire bell rang, the horse hunt began.

In 1858, Chicago's Engine 1 had its first steamer, *Long John*, at the City Armory. The paid driver, Eugene Sullivan, was at hand for alarms, but the horses rented to haul the steamer resided on a farm a mile away. On May 18, 1858, nine people burned to death in a fire only a short distance from the Armory. Shortly thereafter, a stable was built next to the Armory to speed response time. Many horse owners were reluctant to turn docile mounts and delivery horses over to the firehouse drivers for a rousing, rein-slapping *ye-hah* to some smokey blaze only to have the creatures returned singed, trembling, and dazed.

By the close of the 1850s, some volunteer firemen had been through enough battling against the inevitable. One example was the seven volunteer companies of Hoboken, New Jersey. On April 9, 1860, a meeting of volunteers was held in the house of the Washington Hook & Ladder Company No. 1. Built in the 1840s, it was a "storefront" house for a hand-hauled hook-and-ladder truck; the building still exists today as the Hoboken Fire Museum. The meeting was called to form an association of Exempt Firemen of the City of Hoboken.

Their aim was to aid the Hoboken Fire Department and also to ". . . perpetuate the feelings and social activities they had shared as firemen. . ." and now were what was called "exempt" firemen after serving with the department for a length of time. They formed a club of retired fireman who would be entitled to assistance from funds set aside by the department. In recognition of their service, they were also exempt from jury duty and eligible for a "hacker's license"— the license needed to operate a street push-cart to

The ubiquitous fire theme weather vane atop Union Fire Company No. 1.

BUILT BY THE
AMOSKEAG MANUFACTURING CO. MANCHESTER.N.H.

Wm.Amory Treas.
City Exchange. Boston Mass.

E.A. Straw Agent.
Manchester N.H.

ABOVE: The Amoskeag steam pumper was built in Manchester, New Hampshire, and was designed to be pulled by two horses. This 1861 piston machine and its crew of driver and engineer could put out more water than twenty volunteers working the hand pumpers. These steam pumper companies comprised the first full-time paid city fire departments. *Courtesy, CIGNA Museum and Art Collection*

RIGHT: A straight-frame Buckley & Merritt hook-and-ladder truck of 1877 poses in front of the Keystone Fire Company No. 1 firehouse in Reading, Pennsylvania. The length of the truck required a tiller man to get it around corners. Note the fuzzy mascot sharing the driver's seat. *Courtesy, CIGNA Museum and Art Collection*

earn additional retirement income. They could vote on new members and could were eligible to hold public office.

For the retired volunteers, it was a good deal. In keeping with the priorities of most volunteer fire organizations, as soon as the bylaws were drafted, they voted on the design of a suitable badge to be worn by members. On July 14, 1863, a uniform consisting of a red shirt, black tie, belt and fire hat was adopted, and as soon as the war was over they helped organize the first of their parades.

Parades and parties were a priority for most fire companies of that period. In 1864, Thomas Nichols wrote in FORTY YEARS OF AMERICAN LIFE that, in New York City, the members of 50 or 60 volunteer fire companies gave more dances and balls than did 20 or 30 regiments of military volunteers.

By 1890, the Hoboken Exempt Firemen Association had moved into the second floor of the Washington Hook & Ladder Company No. 1 and established its meeting room. That same year, the firehouse was also retired, and the equipment floor

was used as a city garage until it was eventually turned into a museum.

Through the turn of the century, the Hoboken Exempt Volunteers Association participated in a whirlwind of parades and celebrations. They stood by at the unveiling of the Statue of Liberty in 1886, and they procured a silver trowel for the purpose of laying the cornerstone of the Firemen's Monument in Church Square Park in 1891. They celebrated President McKinley's election in grand style. In effect, their club life continued long after their volunteer fire-fighting duty was concluded. And that was the best part of being a volunteer when all was said and done.

By the 1860s the firehouse began to change completely. Driven by the new steam technology, the firehouse was now also under control of civic budgets, bureaucrats, and the need to house 24-hour shift firemen, coal-fired equipment, and the horses. Some hand-pumper houses could be converted, but most had to be pulled down to allow for the heavier steamers, coal bunkers, horse stalls, and feed storage. The

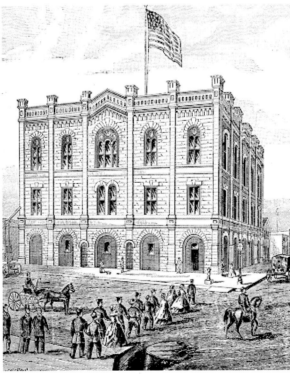

BELOW LEFT: *Long John*, the first steam pumper purchased by the Chicago Fire Department in 1858. BELOW: The City Armory was *Long John's* home, but its first horses were located on a farm a mile away. In 1860, provisions for boarding the first members of the organized paid department were set up at the Armory. This engraving actually shows a round-up of prostitutes being hauled to the cells. Both illustrations, *A. T. Andreas, History of Chicago*

RIGHT: A gathering of Washington Hook & Ladder Company firemen with their ladder truck in the late nineteenth century. After 1890, the first floor became a city garage and today is the Hoboken Fire Department Museum. *Hoboken Fire Department Museum Collection*

LOWER RIGHT: Originally home of the Hoboken, New Jersey, Washington Hook & Ladder Co. No.1, this early form of "storefront" firehouse was sandwiched into its block in the 1840's. The home of a hand-hauled hook-and-ladder truck that eventually converted to two-horsepower, it was turned into the Association of Exempt Firemen meeting hall in 1890.

Civil War stopped the transition process for five years, since whole fire companies enlisted and war needs brought fire-engine manufacture to an end for the duration. But it was only a pause.

Following the Civil War, the volunteers of Southern cities such as those of Alexandria's (Virginia) Friendship Firehouse could only stand and watch as the Union army unloaded their horse-drawn steam pumpers and hose carts to take over the city's firefighting. Some of the fallout of the blood and carnage of that war was the perceived value of steam power in the strategic use of the steam railroads and steam warships that blockaded the Confederate States. Another, far-reaching result of the conflict was the establishment of the battlefield ambulance service. Many volunteer fire companies went to war operating ambulance wagons. This was a concept that took hold in large cities and continued to grow—in fits and starts—into today's paramedic and ambulance service operated by fire departments.

The boys came home from the conflict, and fire

continued on page 67

Following the Civil War, Union troops brought their own steam pumpers and other apparatus to Alexandria, Virginia, when they assumed local fire-fighting duties while occupying key Southern cities. Local residents resented them, of course, but there wasn't much recourse until cities could rebuild.

This view of the Reception of the 29th Regiment at Philadelphia in 1863 shows ambulances bringing up the rear lettered with the names of volunteer fire companies: Hope Hose Company, WECCA Hose Company, Vigilant Fire Co., and Northern Liberty Fire Co. These battlefield ambulances were a product of the carnage suffered on Civil War battlefields. *Courtesy CIGNA Museum and Art Collection*

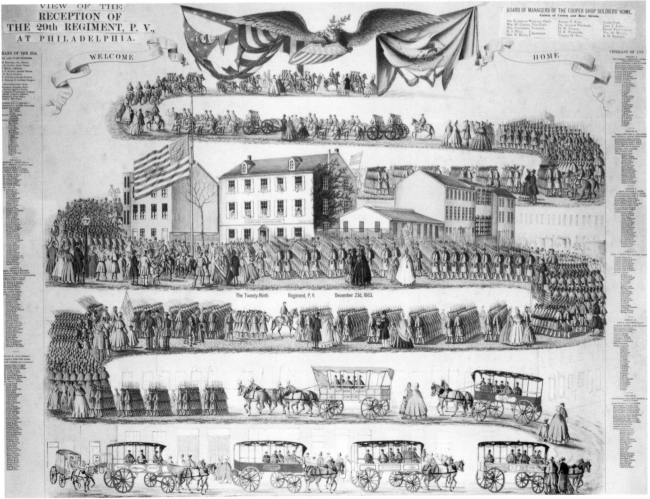

"BEHOLD! HOW SHE SHINES IN HER BEAUTY."
THE STEAM FIRE ENGINE

Ever since Shawk and Latta's steam-powered pumper was tested on January 1, 1853, in Cincinnati, Ohio, firemen's hearts have quickened a beat when they've seen a steamer vibrating, smelled the coal smoke belching from her stack, and listened to the foomph–foomph–foomph music of her pump pistons under load.

That first machine was an ugly affair, a great load of girders around a potbelly boiler and tall smoke stack, riding on three wheels; it was even self-powered. When the back wheels were jacked up, they became the flywheels for the engine. No wonder the volunteers—lying there in the street, blood on their lips, spots dancing before their eyes—regarded the machine that had just beaten their best hand-pumper as a dishonorable opponent. The steamer was simply a brute. Where, amidst all those valves, gauges, braces, and whirling pump wheels could anyone find room to paint a picture of Washington crossing the Delaware or find a spot to hang a crystal glass lantern?

By 1859, Silsby, Lee & Larned, Amoskeag, and Reanie & Neafie were building steam pumpers that had been considerably refined. Knowing their audience, the manufacturers trotted out models resplendent in brass, gold leaf, crystal, gleaming black lacquer, chrome and high-stepping painted-spoke wheels. They were more like carriages for royalty than working fire engines. Their arrival at the firehouse, fresh off a railroad flatcar from the factory, was cause for celebration. Now familiar names like Ahrens-Fox and American La France started out on polished brass plaques bolted to the boiler shells of these formidable machines.

> Behold, how she shines in her beauty,
> Resplendent in silver and gold;
> Ne're shrinking from doing her duty
> When worked by her members so bold;
> So peacefully-innocent standing,
> You'd dream not the work she could do;
> But when we her aid are demanding,
> She always proves faithful and true.
>
> The Steamer! We'll ever adore you;
> In praising you, we never tire;
> Hand engines were nothing before you;
> Nor compared with you when at a fire.
> —The Fireman's Herald, 1882

Like the early Case and Aultman-Taylor steam traction engines that plowed the fields of the late nineteenth century, or the railroad locomotives fresh out of the paint shop from Baldwin Locomotive Works, an engineer accompanied the pumper to the fire company. Learning to deal with steam under enough pressure to pump 1,000 gallons of water per minute, run continuously for a full day, and shoot a 360-foot stream of water was no small skill. Firehouse engineers sometimes learned their trade on their machines working under the tutelage of the factory man, or they came from a job manning steamboats or locomotives. The principals were the same, but the scale was considerably smaller.

For all their virtues, steam pumpers also had two vices. The raw power of the steamer's pump could exhaust all the available water in a pond or well in less than a minute. If the water mains were old and of

Ahrens steam pumper assigned to Chicago's Engine 74 in 1884. Ahrens went on to become Ahrens-Fox, designer of distinctive gas-powered engines that were considered to be the premier apparatus in fire fighting. *Courtesy David R. Phillips Collection*

small diameter, the steamer's efforts were wasted. Large cities such as Chicago, New York, and Philadelphia had medium pressure water mains and fire hydrants by the middle of the nineteenth century. Chicago's new water works built on Michigan Avenue near the lake might have been a factor in extinguishing the Great Chicago Fire earlier had the roof not caved in and fouled the pumps. Smaller communities dug deep cisterns to store water for drafting. Many rural fire company steam pumpers had hard suction drafting hoses with strainers on the end to keep tadpoles and cattails out of the machinery.

The other vice was building up steam in a hurry. Railroads always sent the fireman ahead to fill a locomotive's tender with water, build a good fire in the firebox, and have the engine ready with the right steam pressure for the engineer to take out of the yard. Steamboats also had time at the dock before they slipped their hawsers and engaged their screws. Only the steam fire engine had to be up to pressure in time to fight a fire that might be only minutes away at a fast gallop.

The engineer in a steam-pumper-equipped firehouse had a few options. Basement boilers used to heat the house were furnished with extension pipes that fastened to a coupling and valve on the steamer with a quick disconnect device. Keeping the water in the pumper's boiler warm helps the fire in the firebox do its work that much faster.

Upon returning from a fire, the engineer would connect this pipe to the boiler coupling, then drop the ash and clinker from the fire pan. With the fire grate beneath the boiler clean, fresh kindling would be placed in the firebox. On top of the kindling went a layer of coal in half-fist sizes, then more finely cut kindling called tinder soaked with kerosene. With the fire laid, coal from the basement bunker was brought up in a tin scuttle and the coal pan in front of the firebox doors was filled. This load would last about 20 minutes under full load. Coal wagons were part of every city's fire department. Whether

The steam-pressure gauge of Silsby Third Class rotary steam pumper *James T. Gifford,* purchased by the Elgin Fire Department. The gauge is mounted on the boiler below the builder's plate of the 1869 steam pumper which, with its two horses, were sent to Chicago on October 9, 1871, to help fight the Great Chicago Fire.

delivering to the houses, or at the fire scene, they were critical to a sustained attack on a big blaze.

When the alarm went off, the engineer would disconnect the boiler heater, then either touch off the kerosene-soaked tinder with a long match or employ a couple of alternatives. Some engines had a slow wick pilot light that always burned. As the engine rushed down the ramp, the wick flared and its flame touched off the grate fire. Another trick was a length of chain dangling beneath the firebox. It would strike a spark as it bounced, firing off the tinder. Some houses left a nickel next to the match on the coal pan lip. Kids in the neighborhood knew if the fire alarm went off, the first kid into the house who lit the match and thrust it into the firebox got the nickel.

On the way to the fire, the engineer stood on the rear of the pumper watching the pressure gauge swing up toward its working pressure of about 55-60 pounds. He kept an eagle eye on the water glass that told him its level in the boiler. A low water level could cause an explosion. Since the steam fire engine uses the water-in-a-tube method for quickly building steam, the water must be of good quality. High alkali or dirty water can clog and cause a flue to burst.

At the fire, the engineer is all business, manipulating the input and discharge valves as pressure builds slowly to full strength. Oil fittings and grease cups have been maintained as the flywheels churn faster and the pump pistons work. Black smoke billows from the short stack. Coal or any other fuel that comes to hand must be fed constantly. During the Great Chicago Fire, wood sidewalks and fences were ripped up to keep the pumps going. The engineer watches his gauges, adjusts the valves, tinkers with his oil can, and watches black soot from the stack and ashes from the blaze cover the brass and gold leaf and crystal lanterns of his charge, knowing the steamer must shine as good as new before he goes to bed that night.

THE GREATEST FIRE THAT EVER OCCURRED AT CHICAGO, A NUMBER OF LIVES LOST, AND EIGHT HUNDRED THOUSAND DOLLARS' WORTH OF PROPERTY DESTROYED. FROM A PHOTOGRAPH BY. C. W. LILLIBRIDGE SEE PAGE 350.

The Chicago Fire of 1857 caused $800,000 worth of property losses and the deaths of 23 persons. This fire was a wake-up call to the city that better fire protection was needed and the old hand-pump engine was inadequate—as were the volunteers. *Courtesy CIGNA Museum and Art Collection.*

companies' rosters swelled once again—a phenomenon that would repeat itself until the present day.

To accommodate the fire fighters and new technology, firehouse design went off in two distinct directions: the low road and the high road. The low road, for the most part, was taken up by large cities that needed lots of protection, but didn't want to pay for it—except when it was politically expedient. The high road was slow to start after the war, but gained momentum in smaller communities through the 1880s and 1890s to create some stunning examples of architectural hubris and functional efficiency. We'll begin with an example of the low road taken by Chicago that continued through the turn of the century and still has a legacy today.

Following the Civil War, Chicago just grew and grew, creating a giant wooden firetrap on the shores of Lake Michigan. During that growth—which possibly culminated at the hands of a careless drayman with a discarded match on October 8, 1871—the fire department was the poor cousin of city government. The volunteer fire department that protected Chicago in 1858 had been organized in 1835 when the city was still a town and citizen-fire fighters with hand-pump equipment was good enough. Over the next twenty-some years, Chicago boomed in population and commerce. On October 19, 1857, a major fire killed 23 persons and leveled a half million dollars worth of property. It was time to create an effective fire-fighting department.

As usual, the red-shirt volunteers were flat against the idea of city control and three fire companies, Illinois Hose No. 3, the Red Jacket Engine Company No. 4, and Rescue Hook & Ladder No. 2 were disbanded by the city in February 1858 for demonstrating against the purchase of the steam fire engine *Long John* mentioned earlier. House by house, the city volunteers were supplanted by paid fire companies and horse-drawn steam pumpers, ladder wagons, and hose carts. Since the houses that were taken over by the paid men had no facilities for boarding horses, one can only imagine the living conditions.

Transitioning from volunteers to paid firemen, from hand-pumpers to steam equipment was a new experience for any city. Chicago persevered and dur-

This frame firehouse built for the Chicago Fire Department in 1884 was originally a one-story affair, but the extra half-story was added for a sleeping dormitory and feed loft for the stable in 1891. Mercifully, it was abandoned in 1915. *Ken Little Collection.*

ing the war managed to complete the replacement. They purchased state-of-the-art equipment and began a building program for new firehouses. The pattern for these houses had been carried over from the volunteer era and would stay in place until after World War I.

With minor variations, the houses were two- or three-story brick or frame structures with one bay. The second floor was a dormitory for the men, and the rear of the first floor served as stable area for the horses. Fodder for the horses was kept in a storeroom at the rear of the second floor, hauled up by the bale or sack. The basement housed the boiler for interior heating and, later, for connection by a pipe and quick-disconnect to the steam pumper's boiler to keep the water hot. Coal was loaded into a bin in the basement through an alley window chute. There was no kitchen. The men either brought cold meals or ate at a nearby restaurant. Legend has it that the first sliding pole from the dormitory to the engine floor was invented in a Chicago firehouse in 1878. It was wood with that material's attendant splinter problems. Some bright soul in the New York Fire Department designed a brass version, and that caught on.

The paid force worked as a one-platoon system; everyone was on duty all the time. By 1871, the city was 36 square miles in size. There were 16 steam pumpers, four ladder trucks, six hose units, and two aerial water towers of dubious worth. The theory of the time—and this would remain a basic tenet of "classic" fire fighting for over 90 years—was to dispatch masses of men and water to every fire, often depleting whole sections of the city's fire-fighting capability at each alarm. This worked as long as there wasn't a second big fire, or a third . . .

There was no relief for the exhausted men in the event of a conflagration. This was the case with the Great Chicago Fire of that year. The colossal cost of rebuilding city services after that fire kept expansion down until, by 1875, the department had barely doubled in size to 29 engines serving the entire city. Over the same period, new fire codes for structures were strictly enforced, and insurance patrols kept an eye out for violators and rushed to fires with the firemen to protect insured property.

Manhattan's Engine 54 of the 9th Battalion in New York City is an example of a storefront firehouse shoehorned into a block of flats and shops on a side street. Its red-painted trim and large bay door proclaim its function. *George Proper, courtesy the American Museum of Firefighting Collection.*

An early twentieth-century photo of San Francisco's Engine 11 house at mid-life between its opening in 1872 and closing in 1956. *Ron Mattes Collection*

Some of the houses built after the Chicago Fire had architectural merit including layered brickwork cornices, bay windows, and cut stone decoration, but inside they remained virtually unchanged. While many firehouses were built on corner lots, the era of the "storefront" house shoehorned into a business block had come to stay in cities across the country. These houses usually tried to blend in with the architecture of the flanking structures, often matching the older marble and stone carvings of their neighbors with less expensive cast-iron facades bolted to the bricks. Wherever town centers marched rows of buildings down Main Street in places as disparate as urban Manhattan and rural Hudson, New York, these single-bay houses insinuated themselves. In large cities, they eventually were sold or shut down as the trend went away from using an entire firehouse for one piece of equipment.

Most fire-department money went into equipment while the quality of firehouse construction in Chicago steadily declined until the late 1920s. The building material of choice slid down from brick to wood frame in the mid-to-late 1880s. Although houses built out west and in small towns such as George-

town, Colorado, used frame construction with good results that fit in with the local architecture, the only reason for the Chicago horrors was cheapness—and it showed. These truly cheesy firehouses were finally pulled down after about 15 to 25 years of sodden decay. Uproar in the press demanded that the creaking ruins be replaced, but many had to wait until the 1930s when Works Progress Administration (WPA) funds became available.

Most large post-Civil War cities found their rapid growth was far outstripping their ability to provide services. The "something was better than nothing" architectural plea cropped up wherever business opportunities and population soared. In the American West, rapidly growing cities like San Francisco and Los Angeles tossed together frame firehouses as fast as they could. Engine 11, a particularly dowdy example from 1872, survived the San Francisco quake of 1906 to house fire apparatus for fifty more years.

Chicago wasn't alone in the transition from volunteer to paid, or part-time paid, companies. Most of the major cities' firehouses emerged from the rowdy, sumptuous era of the partying red shirts in spartan condition. City public service budgets had no cash

The P. H. Hamilton Steamer No. 2 house in Coxsackie, New York, makes do without a tower for hose drying. Winter fire fighting must be interesting. *George Proper, courtesy of the American Museum of Firefighting.*

for frills. Cincinnati's Steam Company 19 assembled a house inventory that reflected this makeover:

> One steam engine, one hammer, 1 vise, 10 oil cans, 3 chisels, 1 funnel, 1 jack screw and lever, 1 stove and heating apparatus with platform coal box, poker and shovel, 2 coal buckets, 1 sheet iron smoke stack, 26 feet 3/4 inch rubber hose, 1 clock, 1 alarm... 4 dusters, 5 sponges, 1 mop... 4 leather pipes, 5 nozzles, 1 copper branch pipe, 4 spanners, 3 horses, 3 sets harnesses ... 1 basket, 1 lantern, 1 Bible, 1 table, 6 common chairs, 6 cane-bottom chairs, 6 beds and bedding ... 1 Brussels carpet, 1 oil cloth, 1 bath tub with wash stand and oil cloth, 8 window and door curtains, 1 pick, 1 chamois skin, 1 Thomas cat.

This frugal litany is a far cry from the silver plate, gilded mirrors, and marble tables listed in the 1850 inventory of Philadelphia's volunteer Hibernia Engine Company shown earlier. Also surrendered during this period of bare-bones vandalizing were the exquisite towers, Italianate and Greek Revival, that had topped off the volunteer houses. Hose was now hung in simple racks, or interior cabinets, or draped outside to dry. Lounge rooms with tufted furniture and carpeted floors of the bygone era became sitting rooms with hard-back chairs and card-playing tables. Wood floors were good enough for the recently recruited tobacco-chewing, hard-muscled, ex-army professionals who could rattle a spittoon at ten feet with a well-placed expectoration. Iron bedsteads now lined the walls and— if we go by the Cincinnati inventory head count—six men shared one bathtub (presumably not at the same time).

Gaudy parade costumes and the red shirts of the volunteers also faded away as Union blue became favored by the postwar city governments. What had been feared by municipalities who traded volunteers for professionals was a lack of that enthusiasm that drove the red shirts. Would the professionals display the Èlan of the competing volunteer companies in putting out blazes? This concern turned out to be a non-issue as shown by the subsequent disciplined, courageous, and efficient performance of professional departments throughout the country.

The competition between volunteer companies had also extended to firehouse design. This "our house is grander than yours" attitude continued in smaller cities and towns through the turn of the century. While large cities chose uniformity in design when possible, small towns turned to their business communities for funds, or the volunteers themselves passed the hat. The result of volunteer companies in rural communities competing to build the most elegant firehouses and the communities themselves choosing to focus their civic pride on the sumptuousness of their public buildings—notably the firehouse—was an escalation of self consciousness that rode the architectural high road.

Union Fire Company No. 1, Carlisle, Pennsylvania

Volunteer firemen of the Union Fire Company No. 1 in Carlisle, Pennsylvania, watched the finishing touches being added to their new home from their latest "temporary" quarters across the street. The year was 1869, and the new house was a glorious sight to behold. After all, the community had given builder Benjamin Funk $9,000 to erect it, and that was quite a pat on the back to these itinerant volunteers who were anxious to move in.

The volunteer tradition in Carlisle had begun as

early as 1776 with a loose organization of bucket tossers, but was made official with an "Articles of Agreement" in 1789. A total of 70 people signed these Articles, which were patterned after those of the Union Fire Company of Philadelphia, founded by Benjamin Franklin. The company was charged with not only extinguishing fires, but also preserving the goods and effects of those in danger. With the Articles signed, the company took official possession of a "fire engine" that had been in Carlisle prior to the American Revolution. Most likely, it was a bucket-filled hand-pumper.

Their first house was built in July 1789, a frame and weatherboard shed costing $20. It housed their aging pumper and eight ladders and was located next to the courthouse. The shed lasted until 1821 when it was razed for a two-story station on the same spot. On March 24, 1845, this station burned down and virtually all of Carlisle's fire-fighting equipment was lost. The company borrowed a hand pumper from the Hope Fire Company in Harrisburg until a new engine and hose carriage arrived five months later.

For 14 years, the nomadic company held its meetings in the courthouse and shared a shed with the Cumberland Fire Company for the equipment until

A little innocent card-playing in the Elgin (Illinois) Fire Barn's upstairs recreation room—until you notice the fellow with the dollar bill in his hand looking to buy his way into the game. *Elgin Fire Barn No. 5 Fire Museum Collection.*

Union Fire Company No. 1 of Carlisle, Pennsylvania, and its commemorative arch during the 1789–1889 Centennial Anniversary. Notice the names of the "Visiting Firemen" from surrounding communities on the sides of the archway. Visiting other companies was grand recreation for the volunteers. Parading, drinking, eating, dancing. and contests were all part of the event.

Interior view of the stained glass window that looks into the upstairs meeting room of the Union Fire Company No. 1. An elegant portrayal of ordinary street "furniture!"

Attached to the Union Fire Company No. 1 Museum building is a modern addition built in 1976 for the 3-5 full-time firemen and volunteer company. The house next door is for the chief and the family of one of the fire fighters.

the men could move into a two-story brick building serving as makeshift quarters. There, they dwelled for another 10 years until they could wheel their "squirrel-tail" hand pumper across the street to the grand new edifice that would be their home from then until today.

The firehouse of Union Fire Company No. 1 is a plain, brick, two-story building with white trim windows attached to a facade that must have used up half the building's budget. This facade's explosion of textures and materials is pure Victorian hoopla that makes you smile when you take it all in.

The red-shingled hose tower anchors the right front corner and is balanced by a little turret on the left with little spike on top. Sheltering the fire bell is an open white cupola beneath a brass weather vane. A molded terra-cotta decorative panel is inlaid into the brickwork beneath the cupola, and below that is a stained-glass window depicting a fire hydrant. Originally, stained glass was also part of the bay doors. Chocolate-colored quoins—brick wrapping around corners—run down both sides of the brick tower and the color is repeated over and around all the window and door apertures. The second-floor meeting room looks out on West Louther Street through three windows combined in an arch and past a decorative iron balcony fastened to the building's front with bolts and brackets.

This was state-of-the-art architecture in a rapidly industrializing nation where the urban landscape was becoming heavily pierced with spires and towers. It announces the rediscovery of brick as a "modern" building material and predicts the rapid departure from the white purity of Classic Greek and Colonial styles to the variegated textures of the extremely cluttered Victorian lifestyle.

Union Fire Company No. 1 continued to haul its hand pumper and hose carriage up to 1889 in time for the company's centennial when a Silsby Steam pumper was purchased. The stout lads then hauled the steamer and hose carriage by hand until, tired of beating their feet on Carlisle's cobbles since 1789, or because of the city's demands, horses were added to the roster in 1909. The nags' term of service was so short that there was no time to ennoble them with Victorian sentiment. The firehouse was motorized in 1913 with an American La France engine. The boys of the Union Fire Company No. 1 were state-of-the-art once again.

In 1976, the six-bay addition—three out front and three opening into the alley—was added. Its architecture follows a less flamboyant style, but does tip its

hat to the original with a bit of arched brick and keystone trim together with an equally ornamental iron railing across the three windows above the bays. The company is still comprised of volunteers with full-time paid drivers on duty at the station. Of their five pieces of equipment, the "Four Guys Rural Tanker" made from a stretched Mack trailer tractor is the most unique. It holds 2,000 gallons of water for fires in the rural countryside where no hydrants exist. Working with the tanker is a 1992 Seagrave pumper dubbed "Guns 'n' Hoses."

The original firehouse is now a museum and houses considerable fire memorabilia including the original 1913 American La France engine. Its second floor is still used as a meeting room for the volunteers and holds many mementos of the days when being a volunteer fireman meant having a strong back and a really good pair of running shoes.

LAUREL/REX FIREHOUSES OF 1877 AND 1888

In 1877, the good burghers of York, Pennsylvania, were looking for a home to house the Laurel Fire Company No. 1 and its fire engine. This company traces its origins back to 1770, when it was organized under the title of the Sun Fire Brigade of Yorktown;

TOP: Union Fire Company's Four Guys 2,000-gallon tanker was originally a 1973 Mack tractor trailer that had its frame stretched out in 1985. ABOVE: Union Fire Company purchased a Seagrave pumper in 1992 and dubbed it "Guns 'n' Hoses."

ABOVE: A charcoal sketch of the original Laurel Fire Station made from period photos, drawings, and plans. The soaring wooden bell tower cupola with its ornamental ironwork, flagpole, and weather vane was being repaired at the time the building was photographed for this book. *James Ramsden, York, Pennsylvania.* ABOVE RIGHT: The ever-vigilant owl was the symbol of the Laurel Fire Company and roosts above the Greek Revival capped and pillared bay door—but only on the Laurel side.

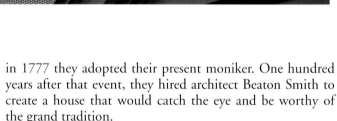

in 1777 they adopted their present moniker. One hundred years after that event, they hired architect Beaton Smith to create a house that would catch the eye and be worthy of the grand tradition.

His answer was a spectacular Victorian creation that used up every trend of the time. Brick was the material of choice because the humble material had been gaining status cloaking opera houses, office buildings, industrial structures, and the big-shouldered fire barns that were just coming into vogue such as the Ann Arbor, Michigan, Fireman's Hall built five years later. Red brick and vertical chocolate brick quoins with matching cast iron and plaster trimmings marched around the building. The mansard roof was supported by brackets and, in turn, was festooned with a pointy iron fence.

With the same Victorian spirit as the Union Fire Company's 1869 house over in Carlisle, and for no apparent good reason other than effect, the hose/bell/watch tower was pushed from its usual position at the back of the house to stage front. The tower was then capped with a soaring white wooden cupola pierced with pointed gothic arch openings, topped off with more pointy ironwork, a flag pole, and a weather vane. The Laurel firehouse is a textbook example of mixed Italianate-Victorian Gothic parentage

The Laurel/Rex Fire Station in York, Pennsylvania, is the composite of two volunteer stations. The Laurel Fire Company No. 1—an engine company—was built in 1877 and incorporated the picturesque patterns and textures of colored stone and brick decorating then found in contemporary public buildings. Later, in 1888, the Rex Ladder Company was looking for a home and was joined at the hip to the Laurel.

With a tower of its own to balance the hose tower of the Laurel station, the Rex Ladder Company's addition followed the multicolored treatment of its mate from window caps to Italianate corbeled overhangs. The structure is a quaint grab-bag of European architectural tricks of the late nineteenth century.

with chocolate and cream Swiss chalet paintwork dropped into the pot for good measure. Beneath its owl mascot over the bay door is emblazoned their motto: Spectamor Agendo: "Let Us Be Judged By Our Actions."

Ten years later, the Rex Hook & Ladder Company was looking for a home. Since the Rex Company got along well (they didn't try to beat each other's brains out at the fire scene) with the Laurel boys, it was decided to expand the Laurel's design to include the Rex house. Though the Rex lads had no hose to dry, they got a consolation tower of their own and a slightly different bay treatment (plain, no columns). Their fraternity had its bounds, however. The line of brick running down between the two bays meant business. Not until 1956 was an interior door added to connect the two companies. Today, only that one small door remains, but the two houses operate as a single entity, Station No. 1.

The second floor is divided into a high-ceilinged meeting room—keeping the custom of the volunteer houses that prevailed through the turn of the century—and a rear dormitory area with lockers. A narrow, creaking stairway clings to one wall and leads to the tall doors that are opened with an old-fashioned key. The meeting room retains some of its furniture including three black chairs sporting carved crossed-hose nozzles behind a formidable black table with a green deal inlay. A brass Laurel hooty-owl peers steadily at attendees from atop the center chair. Hanging from the high ceiling is train wreck of a chandelier sprouting wires, globes, floral glass, tree branches, entwined ivy, and empty sockets.

For all of its tossed-salad architectural effects, the Laurel-Rex Fire Station No. 1 is well-preserved, if fussy, old woman who has aged very well to soar high and gracefully above its neighborhood.

A head-on view of the Laurel/Rex Fire-house shows the use of alternate colored brick in unusual vertical patterns. The line between the stations is no joke. Until 1956, there was no interior door between the volunteer companies and fraternization was held to a minimum except on the fire scene. Today, Laurel/Rex is simply "Station No. 1."

A centrifugal steam pumper and its crew pose in front of Engine House No. 5 at Grand Rapids, Michigan, in the late nineteenth century. *Courtesy Allendale Fire Museum, Allendale, Michigan.*

ENGINE HOUSE NO. 5, GRAND RAPIDS *AND* ALLENDALE, MICHIGAN

To understand how one firehouse can be located in two places some 30 miles apart, you can read the accompanying side bar ("Restoring the Allendale Fire Museum"). Built in 1880 in Grand Rapids, Michigan, on the bank of the Grand River, Engine House No. 5 served the community with a horse-drawn steam pumper and a hose cart. At the time of her construction, she gleamed in white brick with red courses, towered and turreted in almost Byzantine splendor. A great deal of small-town pride was taken in her dazzling architecture and in her horse-drawn steamers.

Matched teams of white and Apaloosa horses drew the steamers to hot and smoky work in the Grand Rapids community. At the house, a drop-down harness system was used for a speedy exit. Her apparatus was eventually was motorized, as typified by the 1921 La France Engine posing on her ramp, and finally, on her 100th birthday in 1980, she was slated to be torn down. By demolition time, her brick had been painted tuscan red, most of the decoration covered over

Turn-of-the-century smoke-eaters in action. Note that the horses have been led away to safety from the steamer as the engineer stokes the firebox. *Allendale Fire Museum Collection, Allendale, Michigan.*

An engineer poses with his steam pumper, complete with a Hale Hanging Harness invented by Chief George Hale of Kansas City. It automatically dropped down on the horses when they were in position in front of the apparatus. *Courtesy Allendale Fire Museum, Allendale, Michigan.*

with plaster, and her usefulness was at an end. But this once-noble structure wasn't leveled by a wrecking ball; rather, it was taken apart brick by brick and moved. Today, this Grande Dame rests—restored to her Victorian splendor—in the small town of Allendale, Michigan.

Except for a somewhat simplified wooden treatment of her 90-foot combination watch and hose tower, she is as she was, supported by brick walls 24 inches thick on the front and 18 inches thick on the sides. The engine room floor is polished wood, and displays of fire equipment and memorabilia are now where the horse stalls once occupied the rear. Above the stalls was a hay loft, and sharing the second floor was the dormitory and meeting room. The chief's office had its own brass fire pole with automatic shutters that opened when the alarm sounded. Beneath the tower is the watch office, equipped with a Gamewell alarm and an alarm repeater used in fire headquarters for distributing an alarm to other companies. Both rooms have been beautifully restored with period furniture and the former chief's office is a working space for the museum.

Engine House No. 5, in Allendale, Michigan, is an excellent museum housed in a rousingly ornate firehouse built in 1885 in nearby Grand Rapids. One hundred years later, it was purchased for $1, dismantled, and moved to the Allendale property for reassembly. Parked in front is a 1928 Ahrens-Fox piston pumper.

Among the apparatus that is displayed on the engine-room floor is a rare restoration of a Babcock chemical wagon that was popular at the time of the building's construction with both rural and city departments. When water mains were still scarce, or not available in rural areas, chemical wagons carried their own small water supply, forced out by mixing acid and alkali soda to produce pressure.

The Babcock chemical wagon of 1877 is a far cry from the later vehicles that called the Grand Rapids firehouse home. The 1921 La France is part of the fire museum's permanent collection. It served the town for 40 years and has been fully restored to running condition. Sharing the engine-room display area is a 1928 Ahrens-Fox pumper—also fully restored to running and pumping condition—whose aristocratic fighting face mirrors the architectural bombast of Engine House No. 5.

Engine House No. 5's reassembly in Allendale included the restoration of a chief's office to its 1880s-era appearance. Surrounded by its polished railing, the brass sliding pole offered a quick exit to the engine room below. *Courtesy Allendale Fire Museum, Allendale, Michigan.*

This photo taken in 1872 outside Hose No. 6 and Engine 19's firehouse at Chicago shows a Babcock chemical wagon carrying two 60-gallon water tanks. Bicarbonate of soda was dissolved into them and acid was added to form a chemical pressure that forced the water out of the slender hose. The suction hose at the rear re-filled the tanks from a hydrant. How did those fire fighters with full beards keep from getting a fast face singe? *Ken Little Collection.*

THE GRANDE DAME OF GRAND RAPIDS GETS A NEW HOME

How does one go about saving a 100-year-old structure that a city government is determined to tear down? Most preservationists stand on street corners with a petition, subjecting passersby to impassioned speeches about the heartless powers who have no appreciation for classic architecture. Some launch a media blitz and, if they are lucky, get a two-minute "sound bite" on the ten o'clock news. More dedicated individuals defy the wrecker's ball by chaining themselves to the building. Few people have the imagination or resources to actually move the structure somewhere else.

In 1980, the city government of Grand Rapids, Michigan, announced plans for demolishing the old abandoned Engine House No. 5 on the banks of the Grand River to make way for a new fire station.

In nearby Allendale, Jeff DePilka, president of West Shore Fire (a fire-fighting products and service company), heard the news and immediately took steps to save it. After much consideration and consulting with experts, he decided that the building could be dismantled brick by brick and reassembled in Allendale, twenty miles away. His offer to purchase the firehouse from the city government was approved with one stipulation—he had to have the entire structure torn down and removed in the next ten weeks. Now, this was no ordinary firehouse. Engine House 5, with its 24-inch-thick front walls and 18-inch-thick side walls, was built to last.

Jeff lost no time in making the arrangements. After purchasing the building for the grand sum of one dollar, he engaged the services of an architect to take measurements and draw up plans for guidance in the rebuilding process. Employees of West Shore Fire and their family members were then pressed into service for the time-consuming task of disassembling the century-old structure.

For the next ten weeks, as autumn winds warned of the coming winter, the workers, under the guidance of supervisor John Bosch, rushed to meet the ten-week deadline. Each day bricks were chipped away, cleaned and loaded onto skids. Trucks ran round-the-clock, transporting the reusable material to the new site on Michigan Avenue in Allendale.

Naturally, a project of this magnitude wasn't without its discouraging moments. Sometimes a worker would spend 30 seconds cleaning a brick by tapping it with a hammer, only to have the brick break with the last tap. Fortunately, because of the thickness of the walls, there were enough spare bricks for replacement. Removing the roof presented another problem. Since it had been a poured tar roof, the men could only beat at it with sledge hammers early in the morning when the air was coldest. Many of the workers suffered severe eye irritation during this process because of the gases that had accumulated with-

ABOVE: Fall 1980: The first step in disassembling Firehouse No. 5 at Grand Rapids was the loosening and cleaning of bricks. BELOW: After the bricks were removed, the excess mortar was tapped off before they were stacked onto pallets. *All photos courtesy Allendale Fire Museum.*

Trucks are taking bricks to Engine Company No. 5's new location in Allendale, twenty miles away from its original site in Grand Rapids. Note how the red paint has chipped away on the original building. The bricks will all face out when the building is reconstructed so as to reveal the original lighter color of the brick.

in the tarring over the years. The most difficult task was dismantling the watchtower, since the bricks were interlaced. Jeff recalls that on one Saturday alone, it took ten workers about eight hours to take apart just four feet of tower. In spite of these setbacks, the job was completed in ten weeks and two days. The extra two days' delay was due to a period of inclement weather.

Little surprises helped keep the project interesting. Prior to demolition, workers noticed that the second floor of the building looked larger on the outside than on the inside. When they searched through the lockers that lined the rear wall on the second floor they noticed that when two of the locker doors were opened, they led to another room behind that wall. That room had formerly been the hayloft, for the horse stalls that were once just below. Old-timers who worked at the original firehouse claimed that, during Prohibition, the hidden "hayloft" saw considerable use by off-duty men as a recreation room where supporters of the Volstead Act were not welcome. This of course, is just an unsubstantiated rumor.

The building elements were stored for almost a year before the arduous reconstruction phase could begin. Workers started laying the bricks for the front and side walls and got as far as the expansion joints, after which the project was halted as winter once again set in. The following February, during a warm spell, they began setting the rear walls in

place. The remaining years were spent putting final touches on the exterior and finishing the interior. To identify the exact location of the original windows, planners examined old photographs of dormitories, and then counted brick courses to establish placement of windows in the new building. Since the original station was painted red on the outside and the finish had chipped over the years, builders turned the bricks inside out to show the original white finish when they reassembled the structure.

The last exterior element to be built was the tower. At this point it was discovered that the original stone for the tower's second level had been stolen, so the final steps were delayed while waiting for the new stone to be delivered. Another setback occurred when a windstorm blew over the top of the tower a few days before it was to be put in place. Luckily, it suffered only minor damage, and the project proceeded as scheduled. The floors in the original building couldn't be saved, but the new building reflected the same interior style of hardwood floors. Unfortunately, there were no artifacts rescued from the Grand Rapids firehouse since it had been empty for so many years. Finally workers completed the building in time for its "grand re-opening" in 1985. Engine House Number 5 was now reincarnated as the Allendale Fire Museum.

Although the building's exterior remains true to the original design, the interior is now a museum dedicated to fire-fighting history, containing rare pieces of equipment and fire-fighting apparatus. One interior decorative detail that many home-owners might envy is the chandelier in the second-floor meeting room, donated by a local Baptist Church. The chandelier was disassembled when the museum acquired it, and members of the church's youth group reassembled the chandelier bead-by-bead—an exacting job made a little more challenging since the beads were graduated in size.

Jeff's interest in the building didn't end after it was rebuilt. For the next ten years, in addition to his responsibilities at West Shore Fire, he traveled around the country purchasing fire-fighting equipment and artifacts to add to the museum's collection. A rare 1870s Edward B. Leverich hose carriage, an 1836 Thayer handpumper, and several 1920s-era motorized engines are among the museum's prized possessions.

Why did Jeff DePilka do it? "We didn't do it for any other reason than to save the building," he said. "It would have been a shame to trash all this architecture."

(From handouts and interviews with Jeff DePilka and Chris Moelker of West Shore Fire)

The steep-pitched cuspate roof is lowered on to the tower at the new site before the tower itself is raised to it commanding position. While still on the ground, workers will repair dents that resulted from the tower having blown over a few days earlier during a violent windstorm.

ANN ARBOR'S FIREMAN'S HALL

To the southeast of Allendale is the college town of Ann Arbor, Michigan. Holding down a choice piece of real estate, sixty feet to the side, on one of its main streets is a magnificent example of the red brick fire barn. Built in 1882, this building is typical of a trend away from small houses scattered throughout a community to the one-stop location for all fire services.

Siting of firehouses was usually governed by availability of cheap land, but eventually basic tenets began to be observed. Firehouses needed to be near main arteries to speed trips to the fire. They needed room to turn horse teams, the high-wheeled pumpers, and ladder trucks after returning from a call. Since downtown businesses usually ponied up— or "invested"—most of the money to keep their insurance rates down, houses were sited at, or within a brief run of, town center. Although high ground was sought when watch towers were an integral part of fire protection, new electrical alarm systems relegated the identifying firehouse towers to the utilitarian duty of hanging long lengths of hose to dry. Having a firehouse plunked down at or near town center placed it on a level with other, much more exalted, public buildings.

In small-to-mid-size municipalities of 10,000 souls such as Ann Arbor in 1882, the Chamber of Commerce and city alderman bit the bullet and put $10,000 on the table. With architect William Scott, selected from a competition, they produced a design that housed a steam pumper, a ladder truck and— in reserve, but also as a sop to the volunteers who would man the facility— the original hand-pumper fire engine. Electric lights would illuminate the interior. Offices were planned for the second floor along with a meeting room, and a hayloft was to be above the horse stalls in the rear of the main floor engine room. When the department replaced the volunteers with a paid company, the meeting room became a spacious dormitory.

Architecturally, the Ann Arbor Fireman's Hall leaves no doubt it was designed from the ground up as a firehouse. Fire helmets and crossed speaking trumpets carved in stone decorate the second floor windows. It shows off Italianate architectural touches from the tower to the arch beneath its single dormer. Carved brick pilasters with vertically fluted panels on either side of the bays complete the menu. The tower swells out at the top and is pierced with iron grillwork and topped with a weather vane. Hydrant top stonework crowns pillars that stand out in relief

Fireman's Hall in Ann Arbor, Michigan, features many different architectural details but is based around an Italianate design. Built in 1882, this red brick firebarn housed all of Ann Arbor's fire equipment at that time. It made use of electric light and other state-of-the-Victorian-art details to mark it as a thoroughly modern structure.

RIGHT AND BELOW: To leave no doubt about the building's intended use, Ann Arbor's Fireman's Hall features fire-fighting details carved into stone relief panels above the windows, and the building's official function is announced in a purely decorative dormer beneath a brick arch. Beautiful brickwork patterns and sculpting are typical of the best of this late nineteenth century period.

across the house's front. Fire-fighting symbolism is everywhere.

Fireman's Hall is a well-proportioned building that clings fairly closely to a unifying design theme. Not every firehouse was quite so lucky. Architectural magazines of the period offered copious menus of selected details from European buildings. The bidding architect could select a gable from column A, a dormer treatment from column B, cornices from column C, and maybe slap up a set of bay doors from the list of appetizers. Italianate, Renaissance, Greek Revival, Federal, Colonial, Classical Revival—every style could go into the same pot . . . and often did. The important part for the town burghers was that the final result looked, well . . . expensive.

Alas, the cost of maintaining overwrought excess proved daunting as the buildings aged. The folks at Ann Arbor rented out the upstairs of the Fireman's Hall for Temperance rallies during Prohibition and after a month of meetings had half the town taking the dry pledge. Eventually, however, the old fire barn lost out to progress and is today a community center. But call it whatever you want, even a casual glance at this landmark proclaims that it's a firehouse.

RACINE FIREHOUSE No.3: THE ECONOMY MODEL FIREHOUSE

Not every community could afford a full-blown fire barn to house all of the city's fire equipment. In Racine, Wisconsin, the job was spread over three houses with Firehouse No. 3 being completed in 1882. It was built as a steam pumper house complete with an attendant hose cart and room for six volunteers and three horses. As with many such small town houses, amenities followed during a considerable time span after opening day.

For example, a year passed after No. 3's completion when a steam pumper manufacturer visited and exhibited one of his machines. On seeing it, the City of Racine came up with the cash and moved the steamer in. Coal stoves originally heated the place, and it wasn't until years later that a hot-water boiler was added—and that was more for pre-heating the steam pumper's water than with any nod toward the firemen's health and hygiene.

The horses were, at first, "borrowed" for hauling the steamer and its hose cart. Later, stalls were built into the rear of the engine room, and the upstairs hay loft was stocked. Later on, a Hale hanging harness was slung above the steamer's whiffletree and the horses were taught to move into place beneath the leather straps and hinged collars for hitching up.

Upstairs, the dormitory was furnished in 1883 with cast-iron bedsteads and a wall of closets for uniforms and personal items. The brass fire pole was extended down to the engine-room floor. The lieutenant's office looked out over 6th Street. When originally built, the very prominent and prison-like tower was used as a day and night fire watch station and for hose drying. When the horses were replaced by motorized equipment, the lofty perch became an office, reached by the original iron spiral staircase. The shift to motorized equipment also required the engine-room floor to be beefed up with steel girders.

Today, the classic structure is the Firehouse No. 3 Museum and home to Racine's last steam pumper and a 1930 Pirsch engine. Also of interest is a working setup that demonstrates the operation of the Gamewell fire alarm system.

Firehouse No. 3 at Racine, Wisconsin, was built in 1881. Kept in operation—in later years, complete with rescue squad—until 1969, today it serves as a museum. Obviously remodeled over the years, it still retains its brickwork trim and cut stone touches, even if the tower makes it look like remnants of an abandoned prison.

MOUNT HOLLY RELIEF FIRE ENGINE CO. NO.1

Harkening back to 1752, the Britannia Fire Company was organized in the town of Bridgeton, New Jersey. The only equipment available was the collection of leather buckets kept at the homes of the volunteers. After the American Revolution, in 1787, they decided "Britannia" sounded too close to the previous motherland and changed the name of the company to the Mount Holly Fire Company. They built a shed in 1789 to house their buckets and ladders and that, eventually, became the oldest firehouse in America and today is located next door to their current fire station.

Sometime during the 1790s townsfolk decided they liked the name of their fire company and changed the town's name from Bridgeton to Mount Holly. The town grew, and in 1805 another fire company was organized. With two fire companies in Mount Holly, the Mount Holly Fire Company was confronted with another name change. They chose

ABOVE: Inside Racine's Firehouse No. 3 is the Racine Firehouse and Museum Collection, which includes a 1930 Pirsch engine facing the old swing-out doors. RIGHT: The collection includes numerous alarms, including this Gamewell box alarm once commonly found on street corners. The interior gear and workings are as intricate as a fine watch.

the Relief Fire Engine Company No. 1. This name stuck, and 193 years later it is the oldest active volunteer fire company in the United States. They're also one fire company that doesn't throw anything out.

In 1892, the town that got its name from the fire company built it a fine firehouse. It housed their new Silsby steam pumper and two horses in considerable style, which appears to be basic Swiss chalet, complete with ubiquitous weather vane perched atop the off-the-shelf two-story firehouse. The modern roll-up doors and the built-on addition to hold more apparatus soften the top-heavy decorative effect. To accommodate the wider bay doors, the entrance was moved around to the side.

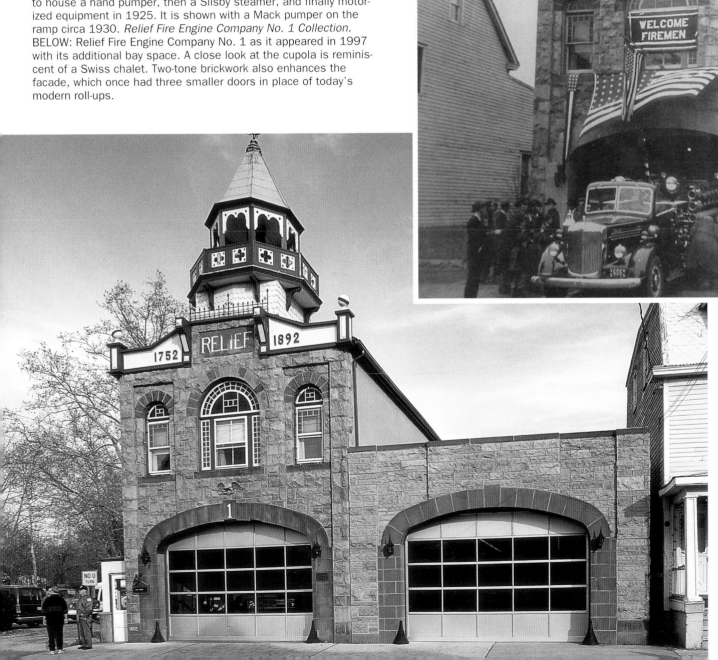

RIGHT: Formed in 1752, Relief Fire Engine Company No. 1 in Mount Holly, New Jersey, is the oldest active volunteer fire department in the United States. Its firehouse was constructed in 1892 to house a hand pumper, then a Silsby steamer, and finally motorized equipment in 1925. It is shown with a Mack pumper on the ramp circa 1930. *Relief Fire Engine Company No. 1 Collection.*
BELOW: Relief Fire Engine Company No. 1 as it appeared in 1997 with its additional bay space. A close look at the cupola is reminiscent of a Swiss chalet. Two-tone brickwork also enhances the facade, which once had three smaller doors in place of today's modern roll-ups.

Fort Wayne Fire Station No. 1 was designed by John F. Wing and M. S. Maharin as an Italianate asymmetrical pile combining a mixed bag of window treatments with Roman arch bays to hold a steamer, ladder truck, aerial ladder, and the chief's buggy. It was the shape of things to come. *Courtesy Fort Wayne Fire Fighters Museum, Inc.*

A small museum is next door to the firehouse, and it contains the original Silsby steam pumper and some leather buckets from the eighteenth-century fire company.

Though this is a working volunteer fire company, the upstairs meeting room is more like a museum, featuring vintage carved oak furniture for every day use, large oil paintings decorating the walls, and artifacts displayed in large glass cases. The room is a time capsule in which the retired volunteers can chat wistfully about the good old days and, as expected, mourn the sad state of today's youth. The company roster has names on it that go back for generations, and there seems to be good reason for the Relief Fire Company No. 1 to continue for generations more.

FORT WAYNE, INDIANA: MIX AND MATCH FIREHOUSES

By 1893, Fort Wayne, at the northeast end of the Hoosier State, was growing at a great rate, and its Third Ward now included the west edge of of the city's center as well as the best residential neighborhood. The town fathers decided to erect a series of firehouses to cover this growth. They turned to the architects, John F. Wing and M. S. Maharin who had already designed firehouse No. 1.

Firehouse No. 1 was an oddly proportioned and asymmetrical building with three arched bays carrying

Fort Wayne's Fire Station No. 3 was a simple two-story affair combining Italianate elements in a two-bay design. It uses pilasters extending to the roofline and a nice use of arches—and one maddeningly square window above the street entrance. *Courtesy Fort Wayne Fire Fighters Museum, Inc.*

Take the design format for Fort Wayne's Station No. 3 (previous page) and mentally superimpose it over Station No. 8 (RIGHT) and you can see how architects Wing and Maharin used mix-and-match exterior treatments over the same set of plans. On station No. 8, everything is squared off with a little balustrade along the roof line. A little quirky, perhaps, but certainly a decent-looking building. *Courtesy Fort Wayne Fire Fighters Museum, Inc.*

Here, the designers have run amuck. The enlargement of Fort Wayne Station No. 3—recognizable on the right—has led to chaos and a cock-eyed building with a mismatched roof and horizontal lines. From the Horse-shoe arched tower that tries to soften the transition between the two wings to the flailing about with windows and trim, they produced a building only the National Register of Historical Places could love. *Courtesy Fort Wayne Fire Fighters Museum, Inc.*

the arch motif to a false fourth bay that encircled the standard entry door. There were dormers flanked by urn-capped columns, much layered brickwork at the roof eaves, and a central tower-cum-dormer that extended down the front of the house and was topped with a semi-circular window. Inside was a full complement of steam pumper, aerial ladder truck, a combination hose and aerial ladder truck as well as the chief's buggy. At least seven horses were also housed within.

Unfortunately, there was an apparent discrepancy concerning the allotted funds promised to architects Wing and Maharin. They were given the bid to design stations 1 through 8 to make up for the shortfall. They, in turn, performed a feat of architectural sleight of hand, squeezing six fire stations and an addition to Fire Station No. 3 from the one set of plans.

Fire Station No. 3 is a not-unpleasing building of two stories, firmly rooted with brick columns in relief. Five windows look out from the second story, and four of them are arched with tip-in transoms. The fifth, above the entrance is, for no apparent reason, square. The roof is a heavy, flat, white-colored overhang that seems to float above a white stone band. A flatbed hose wagon and another combination hose reel and short aerial ladder truck comprise the equipment roster.

Now, take Fire Station No. 3 and lay it on top of Fire Station No. 8 and you'll get a good idea what fire stations 4 through 7 looked like. With a mix-and-match approach to tack-on details, the architects took Fire Station No. 8 and changed the roof overhang and banding details and stuck on a pre-cast railing. The second floor widows are square instead of arched and the square bay doorways have been treated to pre-cast floral necklaces to cap the pillars. The hose tower has been kept in the rear—certainly a lack of showmanship.

As with the Laurel/Rex firehouses of York, Pennsylvania, in 1888, Fort Wayne continued to grow and more space was needed. Here the comparison stops. Whereas the Laurel/Rex volunteer stations could count on deep pockets from local businesses to create a happy blending of the two companies into one expanded firehouse, the architects of the original Fire Station No. 3 hauled out the dog-eared plans that had served so well and created a marvelously cock-eyed solution.

Again, Wing and Maharin dove into their deep bag of tricks and came out with the building—or two buildings bolted together, depending on your point of view—that stands today. One can only imagine the silence in the room when these plans were unrolled. But, the meager budget being met, someone must have said, "It's only a firehouse, not the Taj Mahal," and everyone adjourned for lunch.

A central tower separates the original house from the addition in a vain attempt to mask the differences between the two. Where the original house connects with the tower, an odd bulge of curved brickwork accepts the overhanging roof notch and continues up to the horseshoe-arched belfry. This asymmetry was popular with mansions and industrial buildings of the time. Had they stopped there, everything could still have been okay. They did not.

The recycled plans caused the addition to be least two feet higher than its mate, causing none of the horizontal lines to match up. The addition's roof overhang extends beyond the face of the tower, and its height brings it closer to the belfry. The height difference calls attention to other anomalies. The addition's six windows are only depressed arches as are the bay doorways. In an attempt to accommodate these differences, the tower's center window is a depressed arch while the entry door is enclosed in a full Roman arch.

Looking at the equipment roster arrayed on the firehouse apron—aerial ladder truck, steamer, Preston aerial ladder, hose wagon, and what could be a coal wagon, all towed by a dozen head of horses—it's easy to see there's a lot of space inside. Costs were saved on the addition's second floor, suspending it rather than anchoring it to solid supports as was done with the original. This was fine for a bunk room, but it cannot handle any additional load.

Despite the legerdemain of the architects, Fire Station No. 3 served Fort Wayne's Third Ward with distinction until the last fire run was made on July 20, 1972. Since then, the firehouse was listed on the Indiana Register of Historic Sights and eventually was added to the National Register of Historical Places on June 27, 1979. Today, it is the Fort Wayne Firefighters Museum and boasts a comprehensive collection of apparatus and fire memorabilia—all equipment that once served the city.

THERE'S GOLD IN FIREHOUSE DESIGNS: THE FLOURISHING '90S

Throughout the 1890s, it was evident that architects had realized there was gold in designing firehouses. Advances in pre-casting, molding and the use of steel girder supports on which to hang their polyglot visu-

Engine 28 peeks out of a French Chateau-style firehouse built in Buffalo, New York, circa 1890. The city built a series of these houses into residential neighborhoods with no attempt to blend them with surrounding homes and shops, which certainly were of a more modest style. The idea then was to have firehouses stand out as monuments to the fire-fighting occupation. *George Proper, courtesy of the American Museum of Firefighting.*

al effects allowed free interpretation of the basic design requirements for this unique public building:

⁕An area to store fire-fighting apparatus that allowed quick departure

⁕An area to house the horses and allow for their feeding and hygiene needs

⁕An area to house the firemen, either a dormitory or meeting room

⁕An area (or areas) for offices

⁕A tower or other means for drying hose

⁕A site that allowed easy access to a main artery street and room to maneuver the apparatus

Beyond these basic needs, the architect was free to experiment as long as the town fathers or sponsoring businessmen could be convinced their funds were being well spent.

By this time, the excesses of the volunteers had been forgotten and the public had once again begun to lionize the firemen. This return of public confidence for the brave lads inspired cities and towns to dig a little deeper for new and prestigious designs, lavishing as much budget money on the buildings as they had on the fire fighting hardware.

Built the same year—1893—that the Fort Wayne architects were stamping out look-alikes to save a buck, Boston (Massachusetts) architect Edmund Wheelwright was given the go-ahead to create a ducal palace at 60 Bristol Street.

This charmer in yellow brick translates the need for a fire-department headquarters into a stretch version of the duke's palace in Sienna, Italy. Somewhat excessive for the homely task of hanging hoses to dry, the reason given for the four-story tower was to have a place for the firemen to practice their scaling techniques. Wheelwright explained that the design was a use of European style to achieve "firemanic" requirements. It remained an active firehouse until 1951.

Also under construction in 1893, at Albany, New York, the house being built for Engine Company No. 1 had character of its own. Ernest Hoffman, the architect, clapped together the basic simple forms of the Romanesque Revival style into this symphony of decorative brownstone, dormers, turrets, and chimneys that hunkers down into its site and delivers fire apparatus out of two bays. All that the imposing design needs is a moat. But at the time it was built, this extravagant architecture reflected the esteem the community held for the blue shirts who called it home.

At the other end of New York State, architects in Buffalo were producing a series of French chateaus in pale brick and stone as residential neighborhood firehouses. While Engine 28 appears to be a scaled-down model of the real thing, it serves the purpose of proclaiming its identity with a shout rather than a whisper amidst the more modest neighborhood homes and shops.

The Boston Fire Department headquarters at 60 Bristol Street was housed in this yellow brick Italian palazzo from 1893 until 1950. Architect Edmund Wheelwright lofted up this ornate tower and detailed cornice work that placed the city firehouse on a level with that of a chief magistrate's palace in sixteenth-century Italy. *Ron Mattes Collection.*

Funded by private businessmen, Royal Fire Station No. 6 was a state-of-the-art red brick fire barn in when it opened for business in 1903 at York, Pennsylvania. Its beautifully maintained interior is now the York County Fire Museum and displays a complete collection of fire-fighting apparatus and artifacts. Unique among similar structures of the period, this was probably the last of the opulent volunteer houses built with private money.

CHAPTER 4

A Period of Transition: Turn of the Century to the 1920s

ROYAL FIRE STATION NO. 6, YORK, PENNSYLVANIA

When you approach the Royal Fire Station that fills a large lot next to a busy three-way intersection in this bustling city in the extreme southeast corner of the Keystone State, you can't help but notice the painted statue of a fireman standing high on a pedestal amidst a thicket of trees. The fireman carries a child in one arm and a lantern in the other. As you walk closer, you see a white headstone engraved to "Mac the Fire Horse" (see sidebar on "The Noble Fire Horse"), the original fire bell, and then white marble fire-hydrant castings at the four corners of the sculpture's base. This is the York County Fire Museum now, and these elements are part of the collection.

The museum is located at the edge of a neighborhood of light industry and low-income housing. What you don't see is any graffiti. Nothing is sprayed, carved, or defaced in any way. It's as if this place is out of bounds, yet speaks the same words as the station did when it was new back in 1903. This building and the ground around it is a tribute to York's volunteer firemen, alive and dead, who gave their best for the city.

Back in 1902, a group of well-to-do businessmen pooled their funds and formed the Royal Engine No. 6. The plans were approved and the appointments selected with an eye to luxury. No details were to be spared. When you visit what is now the York County Fire Museum, let your mind go back to those innocent days just after the turn of the century

The exterior is clad in plain red brick with carved brick quoins at the corners of the walls and the tower. Window trim is cream-colored. Brown-painted terra-cotta decorative sills are above the bays and the engine room street entrance. This door is flanked by two lanterns and is beneath the terra-cotta head of their mascot, a lion. The house's motto, Semper Paratus (Always Ready), is lettered around the lion's head. To enter the office wing—that became the volunteers' waiting room in later years—the visitor passes beneath a portico supported by carved wooden pillars topped with floral-enhanced ionic capitals.

If you were to visit the firehouse in 1904, you would enter a wood-paneled and wallpapered hallway. On the left are the polished glass doors leading into the engine room where the steam pumper and hose cart reside. Also sharing this glass door wall is the alarm gong and system. The offices are on the right, and a staircase with a carved balustrade rises toward the second floor. In the engine room, the engineer and his assistant are scraping clinker from the steamer's ash grate onto an old oil cloth spread on the floor. From above, you hear the soft click of billiard balls colliding.

At the top of the second-floor landing, a pair of double doors open into a high-ceiling room where the figured wall paper matches the carpets under

Carved plaster and brass lions proclaiming the fire company motto, *Semper Paratus* (Always Faithful), appear throughout the building.

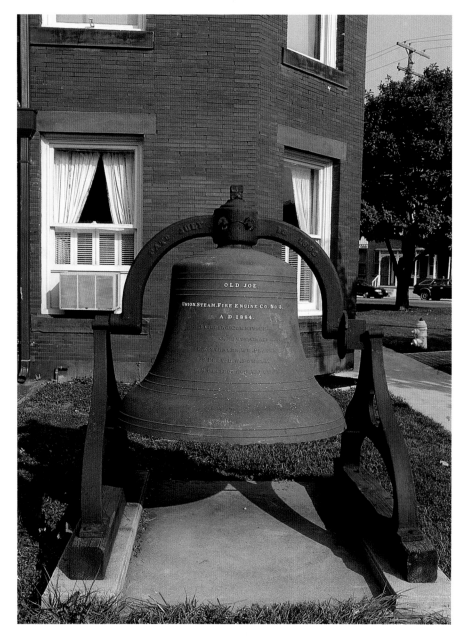

On the lawn of the York County Fire Museum, this fire bell is inscribed as a monument to "Old Joe/Union Steam Fire Engine Number 3/AD 1884"—a memorial to a fire horse. ABOVE RIGHT: The memorial to firemen on the lawn of the former Royal Fire Station No. 6. Its plaque reads "In Memoriam. Dedicated to our heroic firemen who lost mortal life in active service of the York Volunteer Fire Department. *Requiesant in Pace* [They rest in peace]."

foot. The space is large and airy with wingback chairs and tables and features a billiard table where a game is taking place between two men smoking cigars beneath a suspended electric light covered with a translucent green shade. Tall windows cast light across two other men who are engrossed in a game of chess. Where the brass sliding poles intrude, they are canopied, and atop each canopy is a bronze lion mascot and motto. Brass and stoneware spittoons are placed near a green cardtable surrounded by four chairs. A fresh pack of Player cards sits next to the walnut-chip caddy.

Back in the hallway, for the first time you notice the ammoniac scent of a horse stable. In the rear of the engine room, four stable doors—each a Dutch door with an open glass panel—march across the wall. The doors are of carved and polished oak. Hung in front of the steam pumper and the hose wagon are two Hale Hanging harness rigs, suspended from the ceiling by slender cords running through pulley blocks. A horse whinnies and you see "Duke's" muzzle nuzzling the bars in his stall door opening. Behind him, the sound of shoveling and men's voices indicate that the stalls are being mucked out for the manure wagon that will come tomorrow. The engine room smells of brass polish, leather, wet metal, sweat, horses, and freshly turned manure.

Royal Engine No. 6 is a men's club that also happens to be a firehouse. At the sound of the alarm, all the genteel activity will stop, shovels will be downed, and the scuttle of coal standing next to the steamer's fire box will be emptied into its pan. Duke and his three companions, Czar, Prince, and Count, will trot to their places beneath the hanging harness, and in a few moments the pumper and the hose wagon will be rumbling out onto West Market Street, bell clanging.

This is that kind of house. The Royal Engine No. 6 was probably the last of its kind as volunteer stations became more rare in the cities when operating budgets slimmed down. It served as a fire station until 1976 and now is a museum with displays filling its upstairs rooms and the engine-room floor. A 1930 Ahrens-Fox pumper sits where their steamer once quietly percolated waiting for action. Royal Engine No. 6 shows off to visitors from all over the world what the cream of volunteer firehouses were like when we marched boldly into the twentieth century.

What started in the early 1890s as a rebirth of respect for the fireman found full flower in the time between the Spanish-American War with the bully optimism of the Theodore Roosevelt era and the harsh reality of the World War I. The U.S. had beaten the Spanish in 1898, freed Cuba, and found a hero who went on to become President. Roosevelt, America's first "international" President, was a tireless worker, a romantic jingoist, and a hyperbolic booster of the active life. The American fireman fit the ideal of brave manliness created in those optimistic times. His exploits in the ". . . face of the fiery inferno" were regaled in song, story, and eclectic architecture. The most interesting aspect of this worship was the fact that it was directed at city employees, not the self-proclaiming volunteers.

When funds were proposed for new firehouses that included such luxuries as a lounge for the fire-

A solid oak stall doorway looks into the Royal Fire Station No. 6 engine room. The luxurious details of these firehouses included first-class accommodations for the horses as well. The horses were replaced by gasoline-powered engines in 1918, and the area behind the stalls and tack room became a kitchen.

men or a gymnasium for them to help keep fit between alarms, the public's fiscal largess was slow to respond. As a result, politicians trumpeted the moral obligation to support these men. One way or another, some of the truly fine firehouses were built during this period.

ELGIN FIRE BARN NO. 5, ELGIN, ILLINOIS

To celebrate the new year, 1904, the townspeople of Elgin opened a new firehouse, an elegant two-story affair built in the Classical Revival style. Its extensive use of dormers together with the deep roof overhang

mirrored the classical buildings going up along the streets of its neighbor to the east, Chicago. The sheer quality of its construction made it the most expensive firehouse ever built in Elgin. Its total roster consisted of one hose wagon and two horses. By 1888, Elgin had built a new waterworks and from then until 1925 the firemen relied only on water pressure in the mains to fight fires.

The Elgin firehouse design reflects a trend that respected the residential neighborhoods in which these unique buildings were built. While there is no doubt it is a firehouse, but the basic hip roof pierced by dormers gives it a homelike feel. The location is far from downtown Elgin and sits on a pie-shaped piece of property facing out onto a curving front drive that allows entry or exit onto either of two streets. The patch was landscaped from the start with a green lawn and flower gardens.

Fire Barn No. 5 is clad with cream-colored brick and tuscan red brick courses beneath the soffit running in a horizontal line halfway up the building and coloring the overlap bricks that run down each corner. It is crowned with a white wood cupola bell tower, inside of which are inscribed the names of the firemen who finished building the house when public funds ran out. The front has beautiful proportions and is perfectly symmetrical.

The bay doorway was once topped with four glass panels, each criss-crossed by metal strips into four pyramid shapes. These window panels were echoed in a transom above the entry door and window that flanked the bay. Directly above the apparatus doorway is a three-part articulated bay window that is part of the captain's office. This bay continues up through the roof overhang to form a three-window dormer. More dormers march down the east and west sides of the roof, the center one containing three windows. The center pane is topped by a semi-circular window beneath a Palladian dormer. The windows have diamond panes—a motif repeated throughout. All the windows are double-hung against Midwestern winters.

Below this dormer is an elongated bay that runs from roof overhang to the ground and is pierced by one window beneath a brickwork Roman arch trimmed out at the ends with acanthus leaves and parted in the center by a very long keystone. Where the edges of this bay come together, the bricks are interlaced so their ends show.

On the north facade is the hayloft door beneath an arched dormer cornice of its own. The entire haymow door support and cornice are supported by carved brackets. The anchor for the block and tackle is still fastened to the arched cornice overhang.

Inside, Fire Barn No. 5 is outfitted with minimum flourish compared to the genteel excesses of Royal Engine No. 6 described earlier. Since it only housed a hose wagon, the downstairs apparatus floor is pine and needed no extra supports when it was laid. The basement had pegs in the ceiling from which hose was hung to dry. A narrow oak staircase leads to the second floor where the original volunteers had a

LEFT: Home of the Elgin Hose Company No. 5, the Fire Barn turns out its hose wagon for the photographer after its 1904 opening. A new waterworks completed in 1888 allowed the fire department to fight fires with hydrant pressure and chemical wagons until 1925. *Elgin Fire Barn No. 5 Fire Museum Collection.* RIGHT: Beneath its own arched "Paladian" dormer cornice and supported by massive brackets, the utilitarian hay mow doorway that admitted horse fodder to the loft was given star-class treatment. FAR RIGHT: Dormers with diamond-paned glass windows are features of three sides of the house. The wooden cupola was finished by the firemen who signed its interior timbers.

meeting and recreation room as well as an office for the captain and sleeping space for the full-time driver and watchman. The rear of the second floor was dedicated to a hayloft.

The house was shut down in the 1930s but reopened again. Its floor was reinforced with steel girders, and a modern motorized La France engine moved in. By the time of its final closing in the early 1990s, a Seagrave pumper occupied the apparatus floor, and the department was manned by paid men.

Today, Fire Barn No. 5 is a museum and is on the National Register of Historic Places. Its collection is housed on the main floor and its two prize pieces are a 1929 La France Engine and—the rarest of the rare—an 1869 Silsby Third Class steam pumper, the 69th such design built and purchased from Horace Silsby himself at the island Works in Seneca Falls, New York. It was named after Elgin's founding father, James T. Gifford, and cost $8,475 including accompanying hose and reels. What makes this Silsby unique is the fact that it was shipped by flatcar to

Chicago on October 9, 1871, to help fight the Great Chicago Fire (Chapter 1).

After Elgin accepted delivery of the Silsby, the Chicago Fire Department sent out a delegation to see the steamer put though its paces. They were impressed and returned to place their own orders. Two years later, they would see the same machine again drafting water from the Chicago River to fight the blaze that had ravaged most of the the city. The Gifford, operating out of Station No. 1, served Elgin until 1881. Silsby offered to repair the aging steamer for $13,000 and by 1887, the Gifford was finished.

From 1900 to 1973, the machine sat outside in Elgin's Lord's Park where it rotted away. When the City decided to scrap it, firefighters and citizens pooled their money and efforts to have it restored. On August 9, 1981, the *James T. Gifford* was once again paraded down the streets of Elgin.

Every October, at Fire Barn No. 5, the supporters of the museum hold a muster, inviting fire equipment and fire buffs from nearby communities. The

Elgin Fire Barn No. 5 is home to engine No. 2 built in 1929. Regal in handsome pinstriping and featuring a full complement of ladders and booster tank, the handsome American La France-built engine stands on display in 1997 during the annual October muster.

La France engine is wheeled out as is the *James T. Gifford*. Another generation gets to touch and examine classic and famous fire-fighting equipment beneath the shade trees in front of this beautifully preserved old firehouse.

The Classical Revival firehouse was not unique to the Midwest. As far away as the Northwest coast, the town fathers of Seattle, Washington, were also reconsidering their fire-protection facilities. For example, the creaking ruin that was Engine 18 on Russell Avenue opened in 1907 and was shut down in 1911. The beautiful steamer and matching hose wagon drawn by immaculately groomed horses deserved better quarters. Over on Seattle's East Howe Street, a Classical Revival firehouse, Engine 22, opened in 1907 and remained an active station until 1964.

THE DUTCH ARE COMING! THE DUTCH ARE COMING!

Following the turn of the century, architects with firehouse contracts in New York State thumbed through their books of European special effects and came upon the stepped gables of the Dutch Renaissance. New York had a Dutch history going back to the original seaboard trading posts and the great fur trade that managed to corrupt the Eastern Indian tribes, ignite a couple of good wars between the English and the French, and was really hard on the beaver population to boot. This trade provided the foundation money for many a mansion built on the Hudson River. Equating the Dutch heritage with prosperous burghers, a wave of pseudo-Dutch architecture fanned out across the State. Caught up in this wooden-shoe chic were the firehouse builders.

In 1910, architect, Marcus Tullius Reynolds decided to combine fire-fighting theme decorations in a Dutch design that also paid tribute to the fur trade. All this he slapped together for Albany's fire station that would house Engine No. 5 and Ladder No. 1. The result shows that both the Albany town fathers who put up the cash and old Marcus Tullius had a good sense of humor.

Elgin's sooty and battle-scarred *James T. Gifford* had been retired in 1887, but fortunately not scrapped. In this scene circa 1900, she appears to be gussied up for a parade, perhaps. Note the fly wisk harness on the horses. *Elgin Fire Barn No. 5 Fire Museum Collection*

Shingle-sided with numerous decoration details, Seattle Fire Department Engine 22, poised on a Seattle residential street, kept fires at bay from 1909 to 1964. Inside the left door, the engine stands cocked and ready—as soon as the men (apparently posing according to height) remove those Sunday morning chairs from the doorway. *Ron Mattes Collection.*

It is, essentially, a two-bay station beneath a copper sheath roof that eventually acquired a patina of green, as is the case with copper. The copper sheathing extends over a turret on one side and is pierced by stepped gable dormers on two sides. Above the pair of bay doorways that flank the street-entrance door, two stepped-gable parapets rise above the roof's eaves and are capped at their flat peaks with little pedestals. Seated on each pedestal is a green beaver holding a shield. At the side-door entrance next to the turret are two more stepped gables and another pair of guardian beavers. These heralded rodents are a nod to the trappers and skinners of yore who turned the industrious dam engineers into hats and coats.

Where terra-cotta molded sills arch above the bay and street doorways, the fire-fighting theme is kept up by the severed heads of firemen, looking strangely like the Dutch Masters on the lid of cigar boxes of that brand, staring straight ahead.

Around the same time, Engine 253 in Brooklyn was created. Here, the stepped parapets form one end of the gable roof and terminate at a tower made of stepped gables at the other end. All of the house is made of orange brick with horizontal bands of a slightly more red color standing out in relief and circling three sides of the building. Again, the roof is copper sheathed and is now green. High, narrow windows that pierce the tower are more like bow slits where archer snipers could hide. What gives this Dutch firehouse its unusual spin is that the whole

In Upstate New York, Albany's salute to the Dutch includes stepped gable pediments and, recognizing the beaver fur trade, green beavers with shields atop each of the bay gables. This station was built in 1910 to house Hook & Ladder No. 4. *Ron Mattes Collection.*

orange business is grafted onto what appears to be a Norman tithe barn. Its tall, windowless walls are bolstered with full-length pilasters, and the gable roof is covered with tarpaper.

In Chemung County, Engine No. 4 of Elmira, New York, mixes its stepped-gable Dutch look with French diamond brickwork designs, Italianate balustrades, and a colonnaded entry. There is something for everyone—even to the point of keeping one swing-out arched wooden door to co-habitate with one modern roll-up.

By far the most elegant and successful of the Dutch firehouses is the Central Fire Station of Cortland, New York, completed in 1915. It combines the pseudo-Dutch look using horizontal bands of white brick across the stepped gable ends and wrapping around the substantial tower. Five dormers stand at attention across the red gable roof, and beneath the roof eaves are three enclosed balconies entered onto through French doors. Below the balconies are the three firehouse bay doors.

The complete renovation of this working firehouse was accomplished after the city decided that tearing it down and building a new one would be economically unsound. The house's own charm saved it, though it had become sadly dilapidated between its completion in 1915 and its 1979 rebirth. The Dutch styling, so popular before World War I, drew funds from preservation groups and from the Department of the Interior for maintaining fire protection.

Beautiful red brick courses in high relief and a Dutch roof treatment of this engine house in rough-and-tumble Brooklyn, New York, are cemented to what looks like an old Norman-style tithe barn. *George Proper, courtesy of the American Museum of Firefighting.*

Eventually, the renovation was completed without altering the building's appearance, yet it can house modern fire-fighting equipment—barely—considering the relatively low, narrow doorways. Inside, the integrity of the original design was maintained by hardcore preservationists; though when the work was completed, the firemen complained about living in a firehouse on the National Register of Historic Places. Having no air-conditioning and noisy rooms from the high ceilings and hard wood floors, they would actual prefer something a bit more homey.

If Jan van der Heyde, who invented the hand-pumped fire engine and hose combination back in seventeenth century Amsterdam, had visited New York State after the turn of the nineteenth century into the twentieth, he would have felt at home. The bits and pieces of Dutch design tacked together by eclectic architects of the period proved the firehouse could survive just about any interpretation, though later on in its history even that premise would be stretched to the limit.

FAREWELL NOBLE FIREHORSE

After forty years of loyal service, the noble horse faced retirement for good. As early as the late 1890s, when Ransom Olds began piloting his horseless carriage up and down the streets and back roads of Lansing, Michigan, and the Duryea brothers were scorching through Springfield, Massachusetts, the die was cast. At that time, the railroad locomotive was the fastest means of transportation. Special passenger trains were exceeding 100 miles per hour behind their high stepping coal-burners. Except for these missiles tied to their steel rails, the rest of America traveled only as fast as a galloping horse— or maybe the "Standard" high-wheel bicycle, which was both quick and dangerous. (Actually, the great bicycle fad that swept the country throughout the 1890s was responsible for many communities seeking road improvements before the coming of the horseless carriage.)

Engine 4 firehouse at Elmira in New York's Southern Tier region is an elegant Dutch/French/Italianate pile of a structure whose only nod to modern operation is a roll-up door. *George Proper, courtesy of the American Museum of Firefighting.*

Originally built in 1914, this Cortland, New York, firehouse was revamped into its current appearance in 1927 by order of the town fathers. Listed on the National Register, its refurbished appearance in Dutch style houses Engine 1. *George Proper, Courtesy of the American Museum of Firefighting.*

THE FIREHOUSE FIRE HORSE
LOYALTY AT THE GALLOP

Few, if any, firefighters were nurtured or loved in the nineteenth and early twentieth centuries as much as the firehouse horses. Nevertheless, it took several years for volunteer fire companies to accept the horse as part of their companies, because in many cases the red shirts felt threatened—if a fire company had horses to pull the steam engines, it needed fewer men. Volunteers were not willing to give up the prestige and social interaction they enjoyed from being a member of the local fire company. Eventually the volunteers conceded that the most efficient method of bringing fire equipment to the blaze was using a team of healthy, dedicated horses.

In 1887 the Los Angeles Fire Department developed a four-week training schedule for its horses that included

This wonderfully moody lantern slide pays homage to the noble steeds that were always at the ready for a fire emergency. When an alarm sounded, they would leave their stalls, take their positions in front of the hose cart or steam engine, and be on their way in a matter of minutes. *Courtesy CIGNA Museum and Art Collection.*

learning how to back out of stalls at the sound of an alarm, then wait to be harnessed. While ordinary dray horses were first used for hauling equipment, it soon became apparent that choosing the right horse was as important as its subsequent training program. Companies purchased teams of three or four at the same time and based their selections on the animal's breed, strength, and speed.

In 1892 the Fire Department of New York City established a training stable and formal instruction for its horse teams. It wasn't until the following year that the firefighters themselves were given educational facilities. Many felt that the horses received better care than their human counterparts, and the nurturing didn't stop there. In 1906 the department purchased its first ambulance for the trans-

portation of injured horses—before it bought one to transport injured firemen.

This is not to say that these creatures didn't pay back in kind for all they were given. The steeds were ready for any emergency, whether it occurred on a pleasant June afternoon or a subzero night in January. When the alarm sounded, the horses were released from their stalls and immediately took their places in front of the apparatus. There they would wait until the firemen placed the harnesses on their backs (or, in some cases, the harnesses dropped down automatically) and locked their collars in place; then, off they would go, eager to reach their destination. A few high-spirited animals were so eager that they sometimes took off without the engines. Once they arrived at the fire, they were unhitched and led to a safe place until it was time to move the apparatus or return to the firehouse. After they were back in their stalls, the driver or hostler would see to their fodder and water and to work with the hoof pick and grooming brush. Some houses packed their horses' hooves with a special clay that cushioned their feet against the hard pavement. If another fire broke out shortly after they returned, the teams were once again ready to travel. In large cities, veterinary services were a major part of both fire and police budgets until motorized transport became available.

After a firehorse became a member of the firehouse establishment, he was given a name, depending on the firemen's creativity or the personality of the fire company itself. Monikers ranged from the dignified "Duke" or "Prince" to the affectionate "Jack" or "Bill." A fire department in Phoenix, Arizona, used the services of its mares "Nancy" and "Flora" as well as the stallions "Fitz" and "Joe." Firefighters in Omaha, Nebraska, had a more historical focus—"Admiral Dewey" and "Bill McKinley" were well-treated during their years of service.

Firehorses served an average of ten years before they were traded to other, less stressful industries. Some spent their retirement years pulling delivery wagons, but they never forgot their initial training. It was said that the firehorses of the Royal Engine No. 6 in York, Pennsylvania, were programmed to relieve themselves on schedule into waiting shovels. Many a former firehorse, hearing the clanging of the bells passing on a nearby street, laid back his ears, reared in the traces, and plunged ahead toward the sound, leaving a bewildered delivery man hauling uselessly on the reins or sprawling in the dust. Old veteran firefighters had a story about how the Borden dairy wagon was always "the first in" at local fires.

When these loyal equine workers finally passed on to the great pasture in the sky, the firemen's love and respect for them was kept alive in the form of various monuments erected in their honor. The Royal Engine No. 6 held a special place in its heart for Mac, the noble horse of the Rescue Fire Company of York, Pennsylvania. Mac

ABOVE: Mac, the noble horse of the Rescue Fire Company of York, Pennsylvania, photographed around 1900. Mack was a favorite among the citizens of York, even after his "civil servant" days; he spent his retirement years performing "counting tricks" at community functions. LEFT: The gravestone of Mac in front of the Fire Museum of York County. Mack's remains were first interred in the woods just outside of town, but later they were exhumed and reburied on the museum grounds. *Both photos, courtesy of Fire Museum of York County.*

LEFT: A horse known as "Englewood Bill" was used to haul an old-fashioned hose wagon whenever this 1912 Harder hose truck broke down—which was far too frequently for the men's dignity. *Ken Little Collection.*

BELOW: Fred the Fire Horse served the Atlantic Company of New Bern, North Carolina, for 17 years; he died answering a false alarm. Fred was so loved by the men in his company that they had his head preserved as permanent tribute to his loyalty and dedication. You can visit Fred's head at the New Bern, North Carolina, Firemen's Museum. *Courtesy of New Bern Firemen's Museum.*

served the department from about 1884 to just after the turn of the century. Unlike most firehouse horses who were given to other businesses for a quieter, gentler retirement, Mac became a regular performer at meetings, picnics, and school gatherings, doing "counting" tricks. After he died in 1911, he was buried in the woods just outside of York. In 1983, his remains were exhumed and moved to the fire museum where they were reburied—with the exception of his shin bone which is on display in a glass case at the rear of the Fire Museum of York County. A gravestone outside the museum reads "Mac the Noble Horse of the Rescue Fire Company of York, Pennsylvania. Died December 3, 1911." Other steeds of the Royal York had, naturally, "royal" monikers. Names such as "Sultan," "Czar," "Duke," and "Prince" are still engraved over their stalls in the museum.

Firehorse Fred of the New Bern, North Carolina, Atlantic Company of Firefighters was missed so much after his death that his stuffed and mounted head was preserved in a glass case at the New Bern Firemen's Museum. In 1925, at the age of 25, Fred truly died in harness. He suffered a heart attack while answering a false alarm, ending a legendary career that spanned 17 years. It was said that Fred could recognize the tones of the fire alarms and reach many fire locations without being steered.

Some horses were not as swift on their hooves. The Chicago Fire Department's Squad Wagon 3 was forced to use "Englewood Bill" to pull its hose cart to a fire if motorized equipment was out of service. Unfortunately, when an alarm sounded, Bill's laid-back personality didn't allow for any faster gait than a dignified trot. As a result, Squad 3 was always the last to arrive at the scene, much to the chagrin of its crew.

By the 1920s, most horse-drawn equipment had been replaced with gasoline engines, since those vehicles were far cheaper to maintain than the animals who needed hay, grain, and veterinarian services (not to mention disposal of their byproducts) to keep operating. However, even up to the mid-1950s, horsehairs from the Macs and Freds could still be found on the firehouse floors where the stalls had been. These homely artifacts served as a reminder of another era when firefighting teams needed the loyalty of their trusted steeds.

One Baltimore fireman called it quits when the horses were taken from his firehouse and replaced with a gas-powered engine. His wry comment: "There is nothing to it anymore. When they took the horses away, the pep and fun went out of the department. It was the sorriest day in our history."

Fire departments had experimented with self-powered steam pumpers, but the fact that they used up their own steam and coal just getting to the fire made them less than effective. Their primitive steering mechanisms also tended to leave trails of destruction behind the careening vehicle that miffed town fathers and the populace in general.

The transition period was tried in experimental steps. Large cities like Chicago adopted the policy of getting as much mileage as possible out of their inventories of steam pumpers, ladder trucks, and hose wagons by trying out gasoline-powered tractors on the front end instead of old Dobbin. These rigs, built by White, Knox, Mack, and Christie must have seemed daunting to engineers or to horse drivers who had to shift their knowledge from oats, hay, and a hoof pick to gasoline, foot pedals, and a steering wheel. These tractors added years of use to the old steam pumpers and ladder trucks that were kept in reserve long after most fire departments had entirely motorized their companies.

By the time World War I had ended, the gasoline-powered work vehicle was firmly entrenched on this side of the Atlantic as doughboys came home after piloting military trucks through the rutted mud

A steam pumper, hose wagon, and ladder truck pound down a street in Hoboken, New Jersey, near the turn of the century. You can almost hear the steam whistle and clatter of spoked wheels and hooves as the entourage gallops toward the fire. *Courtesy Hoboken Fire Museum.*

At Chicago's Engine 80, a 1917 Christie tractor, has been wedded to a 1912 Nott Doyle steam pumper. This arrangement allowed steam pumpers to be used long after horses had been sold off to delivery-van companies. Note the upright steering wheel—such straight gearing must have built huge shoulders. And how that driver must have missed looking at the backsides of horses after a long run. *Ken Little Collection.*

This elegantly detailed firehouse in South Orange, New Jersey, was designed by architects Arthur Dillon and Henry L. Beadel in 1925 for the princely sum of $70,000. Its numerous decorative details suggest a Norman castle spread out beneath its 90-foot tower. Two Seagrave pumpers and a Seagrave aerial ladder truck are on the ramp.

roads of France. Engine reliability improved along with transmissions and steering mechanisms. All that remained now was to turn the old firehouse horse barn into a garage.

THE FIRE HEADQUARTERS AT SOUTH ORANGE, NEW JERSEY

The transition from horses to motorized vehicles did not occur overnight. Despite the leaps and bounds that technology was making in the private and business sector of America, fire departments were rooted in tradition. Fathers passed along the torch to sons, and fire chiefs stayed on with their ideas about how a fire should be fought for decades after improved methods were available.

While there had been many a heart-tugging "last run of old engine No. 3" behind her galloping span of horses, reality found horses still on fire department rosters years and years after gasoline-powered fire engines were hard at work. Steam-powered pumpers still hunkered at the back of the engine floor in reserve and as late as the 1940s were still hauled out to fight fires when the war virtually halted fire-engine production.

A notable example of the this far-down-the-road transition is the Fire Headquarters in South Orange, New Jersey. On February 25, 1925, the sum of $70,000 was appropriated for the construction of a firehouse. Architects, Dillon and Beadel set their ink to paper and came up with a design that stands today as a beautiful interpretation of the Norman style. Its

Photographed in 1935—dated by the new Seagrave ladder truck purchased that year in the center bay—the South Orange firehouse shows off its Seagrave equipment, the chief's buggy, and, last but not least, its castle-like architecture, all in an earlier, woodsy setting.

proportions are balanced, and it was designed to fit a long, shallow lot that faces out onto two streets by incorporating five bays arranged in the form of an upside-down letter "Y."

Offices are housed in the turret to the left of the three main bays. That feature balances the 90-foot hose-drying tower to the right of the bays. The tower also houses an air-powered alarm whistle that is still blown in South Orange daily at 8 a.m. and 6 p.m. Separate garage bays forming the left and right arms of the upside-down "Y" house the chief's buggy and, today, an emergency vehicle.

Many artists and students come to South Orange just to draw and photograph this elegant, working fire station with its complement of Seagrave pumpers and aerial ladder. What they can't appreciate is, that in 1925, this firehouse was designed to house horses complete with feed bins and hay racks.

Looking at Drawing No. 3 of the architects' plans reveals a pair of stalls in the right rear of the engine floor with room for more. One can imagine as motorized vehicles were bought by the city to replace horse-drawn pumpers, the number of stalls diminished as the plans moved forward from their original concept. Otherwise, why just two stalls for such a huge firehouse?

According to Anthony Vecchio, firefighter and department historian for the South Orange Fire Department, there was another oversight that was eventually corrected,

"You will note that the building was designed without a kitchen. This was because the paid men were given three one-hour dinner times on a rotating basis to leave the firehouse and return. This changed shortly after a disastrous fire in the town. A whole new shift was added and the kitchen was built by the men. Today, the kitchen is where the horse stalls were originally designated to be built."

The South Orange Fire Department Headquarters did follow a typical path from horse barn to garage. Most of the houses, large and small, that once had horses as part of their fire-fighting team built their kitchen in the space once occupied by the stalls. One can only hope the aromas wafting from that location were a considerable improvement.

BELOW: The modern Seagrave fire-fighting equipment seems out of place beneath the peaked dormers and 90-foot Norman hose tower of this grande dame of engine houses.

BELOW RIGHT: Wearing a patina of green, copper gargoyles adorn the peaks of the roof's many shingled dormers. Beneath the peak, semi-circular carved caps top each double-hung window.

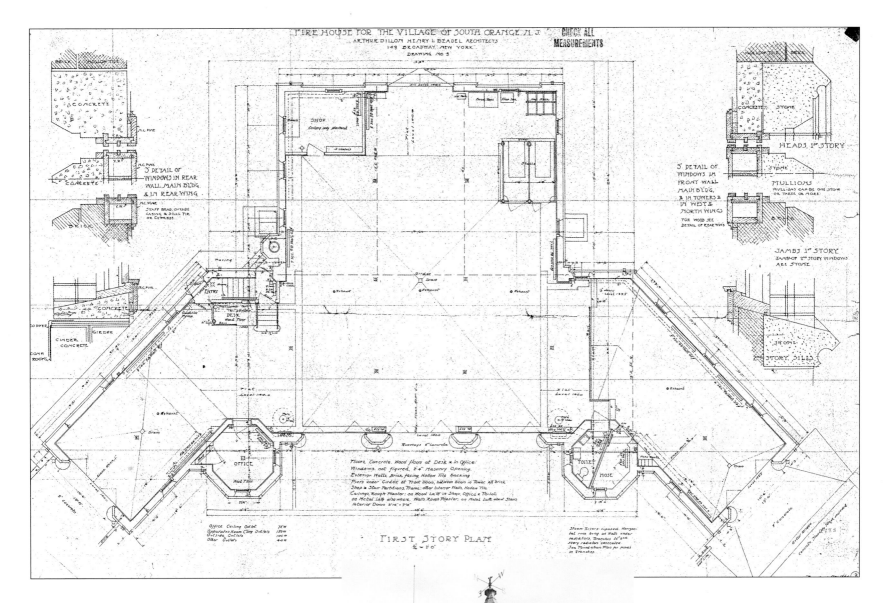

FIRST STORY PLAN

ABOVE: From their office at 149 Broadway in New York City, architects Dillon and Beadel issued this plan of the South Orange firehouse in November 1924. This was noted to be a "revised" plan, and this version featured but two horse stalls, at the upper-right corner of the plan. Nearby were the feed bin and hay loft. This area later became a kitchen. RIGHT: The medieval tower with its vented louvers in place of windows was designed for drying hose, not observation, and still serves that purpose today.

Stately Engine 13 at 1020 Collins Avenue in Syracuse, New York, at first glance appears just to be another cozy home in a pleasant neighborhood. A second glance might have you questioning what the family keeps in that built-in garage whose door is large enough to accommodate a . . . *fire engine*? *George Proper, courtesy of the American Museum of Firefighting.*

CHAPTER 5

The Roaring Twenties: Gasoline Power and a Flurry of Construction

There's a jingle in the jungle,
'Neath the Juniper and Pine,
They are mangling the tangle
Of the underbrush and vine,
And my blood is all a-tingle
At the sound of blow on blow,
As I count each single shingle
On my bosky bungalow.
From "Bungal-ode" by Burgess Johnson

—The American Bungalow

The bungalow was perfect camouflage, if an imperfect solution for residential firehouses. During the first 25 years following the turn of the century, America underwent some startling changes. World War I, Prohibition, and women getting the right to vote would head up most people's top-ten list. But threaded through the fabric of our growing society was the track of the automobile. With it, Americans were cut free from congested cities, from stagnant little farm communities, and from life patterns where travel was a rare experience or was tied to public transport. You could live where you wanted to be, because the car could take you to where you needed to be, then take you to where it was fun to be.

Developers and home-builders cocked an ear to this siren song and soon suburbs sprouted at metropolitan edges. Road-building programs accelerated to keep pace with postwar prosperity of a Ford in every garage. On the East Coast, clusters of little houses began popping up like mushrooms on a log. They were a gift from English architects: flat little houses called "bungalows."

The word came from the Bengali noun "bengala," meaning a low house surrounded by porches or galleries. The British brought the idea home from India to use on second homes in the country or as seaside cottages. Eventually, the working classes adopted the bungalow as their only home.

No good idea could keep from jumping across the Atlantic, and soon, in 1879, a shingled, low-roofed beach house surrounded by a broad veranda (the Indian equivalent of "front porch") was built by architect William Gibbons Preston at Buzzards Bay, Massachusetts, near Cape Cod. From there, the bungalow's basic idea sprouted dormers, a second floor, an attic, chimney pots, and terraced gardens. It could look like everything from a Swiss chalet to a Peking pagoda to a Frank Lloyd Wright prairie house that spread across an acre lot. In other words, it became a frame of mind rather than an example of architecture bound by hard and fast rules as was the case with Greek Revival, Federal, Norman, or even the stretched and pulled Italianate.

The one common desire among all bungalow owners—whether they were crammed together six

A prize of the "Roaring Twenties" is the 1928 Ahrens-Fox engine at the Allendale, Michigan, Engine House No. 5 Collection, whose details shine in this close-up study. Fully restored and in running condition, the engine harkens to an era of transformation for the firehouse.

"Honey, I'm home!" Engine 34 at Seattle, Washington, was built in 1914 and closed in 1970. Today it serves as a private residence—which is what it looked like all along. *Ron Mattes Collection.*

houses to the block or one house to the quarter mile—was to maintain the integrity of their surroundings. Unfortunately, bungalows were not fireproof. They burned smartly if given half a chance, so the need for protection was voiced. But the idea of plopping down a two-story brick-and-stone firehouse into the bosky dells of bungalowland was out of the question.

Once the horse barn and steamers gave way to the garage with its motorized fire engines and trucks, architects exploited the new freedom. A firehouse could look like anything now. Why not a bungalow?

Of all the attributes of the true bungalow, its openness to the out-of-doors, expansive galleries or porches, and the signature big, low roof offered challenges. The first thing to go in many houses was the second story. Engine 34 at Seattle, opened in 1915 and closed in 1974. It would look right at home with a newspaper on the front lawn and a blue-shirted resident hooking up the garden hose to a sprinkler. This is an enginehouse that contained a fully outfitted pumper, its hose, and a crew of at least four firemen. Architects also said good-by to the hose-drying tower, opting for drying closets that extended down past the

basement. Smaller La France engines affixed with 40-gallon booster tanks and a pair of short ladders could fit in the garage bay that looks better suited to a Hupmobile Six.

Another officially designated bungalow house was Engine 48 in Cincinnati, Ohio. Here, the 1912 Seagrave or La France pumper that would have been brand new when this house opened, blew out onto Vine Street through a portal worthy of the best stewpot Victorian stage pieces of the 1890s. A look down the strictly industrial side of the building shows how really deep it is to accommodate the apparatus and internal workings. The house was closed in 1934, but its bolted-on Lowes Chinese Theater entrance remains.

It was in California where eclectic firehouse architecture really flourished, embracing the sunshine, the gardens, and the happy eccentricities of Lotus Land architects. In Santa Barbara, Engine 3 opened in 1929 and remains an active firehouse. Here, the going was a little easier since Spanish architecture can support a tower for drying hose and Spanish missions had big front doors, though these arched wooden beauties that swing in probably restrict the size of modern equipment that will race from beneath that

Formerly Engine 48, this ornate and gilded building was opened in 1912 and closed as a firehouse in 1939. It was the first bungalow house in Cincinnati, Ohio, providing almost total camouflage for its real purpose. *Ron Mattes Collection.*

flower-festooned balcony.

Architects, Edwards, Plunkett and Howell were working within a Santa Barbara covenant that all new homes or public buildings conform to a Hispanic motif. Its proportions are very pleasing, and the little sign out front makes tourists aware that there is no wine tasting going on inside.

Being exposed to California sunshine days and months on end must inspire a sense of whimsy in some architects. Oakland's Engine 24 sits on Moraga Avenue like a gingerbread pastry. If any firehouse featured in this book proves the rule that firemen can cope with any character-building situation, this edifice proves the rule. You can imagine the first fire company that reported to Engine 24 when it was opened in 1927 did so with paper bags over their heads. Eventually, pride of place took over and this architectural ornament is now a landmark—even if local residents do refer to its style as Restrained Mother Goose or Hansel and Gretel Revival.

Not all single-dwelling firehouses could aspire to the bungalow label and had to settle for more derivative suburban designs that fit the local styles. The humble cottage on Route 28A in Falmouth, Massa-

chusetts, began housing Engine No. 4 back in 1930. With the garage door shut, you could imaging a tricycle sitting in the driveway, but beneath that bracketed overhang, the red snout of a pumper, primed and ready, looks out, ready for action. This firehouse reverted back to a family dwelling in 1956.

These fire "homes" also provided kitchen amenities to paid crews and the iron-bedstead dormitories were replaced with rooms sleeping two men each. In volunteer homes, the paid driver could actually live with his family—as long as he parked his personal car outside.

One problem that slowed the insinuation of homelike firehouses into residential communities was cost. Since the requirements for a firehouse were somewhat fixed, ways had to be found to fiddle them into a more domestic design. Also, since neighborhoods all had their own "environments," Home Firehouse Design Model 27B couldn't always expected to match its neighbors in order to blend in. The cost of adapting standard home plans to meet firehouse needs often more than doubled the cost for a less-constrained design.

Engine 33, another Seattle native, was built in

WHEN A SIMPLE SHED WILL DO

Considering the minimalist requirements of the Brittania Fire Company in Bridgeton, New Jersey, back in 1798, a simple shed to hold their buckets seems suitable, if quaint and old fashioned.

A visit to a few rural countryside locations reveals that this minimalist philosophy is alive and well. For many small fire departments manned by volunteers strung out through the hills, often all they need is a place to store their apparatus. The late George Proper, volunteer fire historian for the State of New York, spent a great deal of his time recording pictures of every known firehouse. During his travels through New York's counties over the years, he discov-

ered many of these basic shelters. Ron Mattes, a former fire-fighter and avid firehouse photographer, also discovered a humble example in Omaha, Nebraska.

Are these any less of a firehouse than the more imposing structures that have seven bays or facilities for a dozen working firemen? We would say, no. They are no less valid than the bungalows that are designed to disguise their function, or that little windowless shed that led off our book and which is now a historical landmark. Grab a bucket, or grab a fire engine. These are the little sheds that could... and do.

UPPER LEFT: Virgil fire station in Cortland County, New York's, fire station built in 1926 is disguised as an automobile garage. *George Proper, courtesy the American Museum of Firefighting.*

ABOVE: Genesee County, New York, achieved the ultimate in minimalist design. *George Proper, courtesy the American Museum of Firefighting.*

LEFT: There's just room enough for "Wendellville Fire Co., Inc., No. 2" above the door. *George Proper, courtesy the American Museum of Firefighting.*

1917 and served its community until 1972. From head on, it appears to be a nicely proportioned, shingle-clad, gable-roof home with a somewhat oversize garage door. A look along its side shows how far that garage area was extended back to house the ladder-equipped Mack pumper poised in the shadows. Add to this the cost of an internal hose-drying system, vehicle maintenance facilities, and upstairs housing for the crew, and the bill mounts up quickly.

The larger the basic home design, the easier the conversion as with the virtually perfect camouflage of Engine 13 belonging to the Syracuse, New York, Fire Department in Onondaga County. Well sited on a tree-clad corner lot, the sight of a red pumper with siren blaring as it swung onto Collins Avenue from the garage of this stately matron must have startled passing motorists.

Firehouse historian George Proper roamed through New York State with his camera and found many local architectural expressions of the growing need for centralization of fire facilities and housing more than one piece of equipment under one roof.

The new use—as a firehouse or perhaps "firebarn," if you will—of an old barn in Verdoy County contrasts with the semi-gambrel roofbarn architecture used in Watertown for a larger operation. In another part of the State, the folks of Chenango Forks in Broome County park their apparatus in something akin to a feed and grain store—complete with Saturday night bingo to raise money for a new fire truck.

The City of Santa Barbara, California, required that all its firehouses conform to a Spanish motif. Architects Edwards, Plunkett, and Howell complied in this south-of-the-border look that opened in 1929. Note the small swing-in doors for modern equipment. Except for the sign in front of the bushes, passersby might stop to sample the wine. *Ron Mattes Collection*

Meanwhile, the problem of expanding fire coverage was solved by the town of Newport in Herkimer County by adding two bays faced with brick and supported by cinder blocks that look as though they were laid by dropping them from a great height. This flat-roofed garage pair is grafted to the side of their charming frame firehouse that has outlived its capacity. Elegance aside, they got the job done.

In time, the art of concealment gave way to more practical considerations. The bosky dell charm of the Brighton Fire Department's Fire Station No. 3 in New York State's Monroe County—complete with ornamental well planter and pseudo-Tudor timbering—were replaced with larger, more centralized houses. Cost and crew considerations began to erode the small houses containing only one piece of equipment. In the same county, the citizens of Brockport opted for a more straightforward solution that manages to conceal two equipment bays beneath a deep veranda that would look at home as a bungalow consulate in Bermuda.

If there was no place to hide in the rural communities, then combining functions into one public building solved the space problem—if not always in the most esthetic way. George paused long enough in Glen Park, New York, to capture a Colonial Revival facade shored up with Greek Ionic capital columns perched atop "modern" back-slanting supports. The combination village hall/fire department is a pocket version of this solution that became popular across the country.

The concept of firehouse camouflage never completely went away following the bungalow craze of our century's first 25 years. In 1952, the city of Waukegan, Illinois, built a two-bay bungalow-style firehouse on a residential street. Its screened front porch and low single-story silhouette tips its hat to designs that went before while providing both pumper and emergency medical services to the community.

By 1975, the flat-roofed, expansive ranch-home design—the honorary stepchild of the bungalow—was adapted by Engine 15 in Lexington, Kentucky, while in New York State's Cole County a six bay firehouse masquerades as either a Howard Johnson

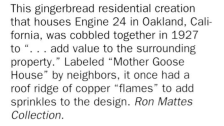

This gingerbread residential creation that houses Engine 24 in Oakland, California, was cobbled together in 1927 to ". . . add value to the surrounding property." Labeled "Mother Goose House" by neighbors, it once had a roof ridge of copper "flames" to add sprinkles to the design. *Ron Mattes Collection.*

Seattle's Engine 33 was residing in this "home" when it closed as a firehouse in 1972. When built in 1917, it was the height of style. *Ron Mattes Collection*

restaurant with its bright orange portico or a gas station sans pumps.

The growth of the high-rise drew some designers to created "service-integrated buildings," placing fire facilities within these vertical complexes by assigning a portion of the ground floor to a fire-fighting company. In Binghamton, New York, Fire Station No. 5 looks for all the world like a colorful parking lot. Over in Wheeling, West Virginia, the fire department headquarters and Engine No. 8 peek out of their corner of the concrete jungle that opened in 1978. Matching high-rise architecture in the 1970s was also the design concept behind the home of Engine No. 11 in Fort Lauderdale, Florida. It is a flat-roofed mirror image of the condo complex behind it.

The return to large firehouses containing a variety of apparatus—but with a need to "blend in" with community architecture—has been kept up into the 1990s. The Village of Lake Forest, Illinois, built this Everett Road "fire barn" in 1993. A Pierce fire engine of Engine 215 sits on the apron in front of one of the three bays. The house is sited next to the Metra commuter-train main line amidst asphalt parking lots. At times, persons looking for the local depot have entered the firehouse to get their tickets. What qualifies this house for inclusion here is the fact that its entire second floor is false. This is a single-story fire-

house with a meeting room in the basement. It is such a prominent building that the town fathers thought it should reflect the surrounding Colonial architecture; hence the fake roof and fake dormers.

In the Village of Lake Zurich, Illinois, this half-timbered, gambrel-roofed, Tudor-ish firehouse also resorted to architectural deception. In 1933, the first volunteer department was built downtown, but as the suburb grew, greater coverage was needed. A flat-roofed house was constructed on this site in 1981 to store equipment for the paid-on-call department. Within seven years, growth had once again forced the department to increase its capabilities. Shifts were realigned so that 13 firefighters were on duty at all times with a shift commander and two lieutenants. By 1988, emergency paramedics were added to the roster. These additions required expanding this Lake Zurich house's facilities to include more amenities for the blue shirts including a full kitchen and common room, a three-story training tower, and a roof simulator for ventilation training. Rather than pull down the 1981 station, it was expanded in 1990, and a new roof was added. The entire half-timbered second story is false to blend in with local architecture of the encircling housing developments.

The need for fire protection—but not at the cost of marring the ambiance of the local architecture—continues its search for solutions. The sensibilities of the

This "fire barn" was home to the Emergency Services station of Verdoy, New York. Here was one reuse of a barn in which the barn doors were just the right size! *George Proper, courtesy the American Museum of Firefighting.*

The checkerboard door on the Chenango Forks, New York, Fire Department looks like a feed-store entrance. When fire fighting slacks off, there's always the Bingo game upstairs. *George Proper, courtesy the American Museum of Firefighting.*

new suburban bungalow owners back in those optimistic 25 to 30 years following the turn of the century are still in force. But during that same time period, builders and architects in the big cities were thinking on a grander scale.

PUTTING ON A MODERN FACE: THE UNFETTERED FIREHOUSE

Chicago's beloved horses made their last run on February 5, 1923, to a box alarm at a downtown street corner. And that was that. Chicago was totally motorized.

The road to modernization would still be a long haul. Almost all of the brand-new gas-powered apparatus would continue to operate from houses built as horse barns through World War II, and many of these ancient piles are in use today. As the role of government came under the control of more specialists and more college-trained planners, the face of America's cities began to change.

Where once the firehouses and police stations were located near downtown center, later time-saving surveys found that being outside urban congestion with access to fast main arteries was more important. The shift to

The wedding of the village hall (upstairs) to the fire department (downstairs) at Glen Park, New York, nails Greek Revival onto the front of a style you might call "Suburban Confusion." *George Proper, courtesy of the American Museum of Firefighting.*

Station 5 in Binghamton, New York, resembles a parking ramp for fire engines while serving out its function as part of a multi-purpose building. So much for esthetics. *George Proper, courtesy the American Museum of Firefighting*

1880s had been wooden one- and two-story affairs punched from a pattern. Following World War I, these unsightly and teetering stick structures were all over the cityscape like a rash. Their replacement would have to wait for the fall-out from Prohibition. William Hale Thompson—a.k.a "Big Bill" or "Big Bill the Builder"—was elected Mayor of Chicago in 1915. During the War, he was pro-German and anti-British, going as far as having public book burnings of pro-British books. The people of Chicago re-elected him in 1919. By 1923, everyone was tired of "Big Bill" and upon learning that he was the subject of an investigation for fraud, he bolted from the 1923 election. Persuaded by the booming profits to be made during Prohibition and encouraged by his chums, Johnnie Torrio and Al Capone, he ran again in 1927 and was elected.

No sooner was he back in office than the *Chicago Daily News* ran a series of articles pointing out the sad condition of the city's old wooden firehouses. A bond issue was pending to secure money for replacing them and the press ballyhoo rallied support. Seeing an issue that called on one of his real skills—spending money—Thompson looked out of Capone's pocket long enough to start a firehouse-building program with the bond money that produced some of the city's most eccentrically beautiful stations. By 1931, he had once again out-stayed his welcome and lost to Anton Cermak. Today, Thompson lies in Chicago's Oak Woods Cemetery next to a tall stone shaft erected in his name. This monument symbolizes what Big Bill Thompson frequently gave to the people of Chicago.

motorized vehicles and their faster sustainable speed allowed them to be housed further from heavily built-up commerce and government centers. With this being the case, the small, single-bay houses were sold off and larger, multi-unit stations like the five bay Fire Headquarters at South Orange, New Jersey (previous chapter) were being built. As regulations—for example, the 1923 State Zoning Enabling Act passed by the Commerce Department—restricted industrial growth and established inviolate residential and park areas, siting firehouses became easier for planners.

For large, densely populated cities like Chicago and New York City, the problem was not so easily solved. In Chicago, light industry and residential neighborhoods were cheek by jowl, and "ward healers"—as the Aldermen were called—could not support closing any of the firehouses that existed. Since the huge growth spurt that had occurred following the Great Chicago Fire, a large number of small, single-bay firehouses had been built. Many during the

On the plus side, Bill's most visible legacy is a collection of seven flappers that were the bees knees as the 1920s drew to a close. A perfect roll of the dice that Big Bill the Builder left behind is his "English of the Stuart Period" style. His architectural largess was only surpassed by his contemporary, New York's Mayor Jimmy Walker. "Beau James" slapped up 23 new stations for his political pals, the firefighters. He would have built 17 more, but he had to resign in 1932 after being accused of accepting over a million dollars from the construction companies. Curiously, they all opened in 1928 and 1929—during the last gasp of our economy before the Great Depression took hold.

In overall style, they each try to elbow the other out of the spotlight for points awarded to eccentric ornament, but the family resemblance is unmistakable. As with the Fort Wayne (Indiana) go-for-cheap blueprint re-cycling program discussed earlier, it seems that two sets of plans were all that was needed for five of the houses.

Engine 65, Engine 45, and Engine 129 are more than kissing cousins. These two-bay houses show three facade variations using red brick, white stone, and big red doors. Engine 45, opened in 1928, and Engine 65, finished in 1929, are fortunate that they are on corner lots so their side trimming can be enjoyed from two different streets. Engine 129, on the other hand, had its "English in the Stuart style" facade bolted onto ho-hum side walls for its 1929 debut.

When Truck 47 became the Painted Lady of North Ridge Avenue in 1929, it was evident that no expense had been spared. Argyle E. Robinson, the architect, put together a plan that kept every stone mason in town who could lift a chisel working and in debt to Big Bill. The house was built for motorized vehicles and was one of the first to have doors that opened automatically. For anyone who wanted to travel to the other end of the city, they could find the mirror image of Truck 47, but it housed Engine 61. This firehouse opened in 1928 and uses the stone

The affluent Chicago suburb of Lake Forest, Illinois, created this elegantly proportioned fire station and office block to blend into the neighborhood. Its Greek Revival roof line covers a false second floor. In reality it's a one-story house with a basement meeting room and living quarters. A Pierce fire engine rests on the ramp.

Lake Zurich, Illinois—another Chicago suburb—houses part of its paid and paid-on-call department in this simulated Tudor, half-timbered station. To better blend into residential area, the original flat-roofed storage house built in 1981 was remodeled with this false second floor in 1990.

mason's craft with some restraint and in proportion to the building's mass. It displays the innocence of your basic two-story firehouse dressed up to go to the prom. Truck 47 seems to have been an attempt to "up the ante" when it was discovered there was a lot of stone left over. Her prom days are long behind her.

The two truly unique houses that emerge from this orgy of troweled-on decor are Truck 51 and Engine 5. They are larger buildings and though variations on Engine 5's four-square design are common in cities across the country, here the white stonework quoins seem like a gift to relieve the punched-out sameness of three bays and two stories on a corner lot. Truck 51 is the best of the lot. In 1928, the archi-

tect used the white stone quoins to enhance the height of the two towers that flank the Roman arch front bay. If it was made of rough-hewn stone, it would be Romanesque in the style of the Albany (New York) firehouses-as-fortresses discussed earlier. Its proportions are pleasantly symmetrical, and the banded chimney that rises at the rear of the building does not look at all out of place. Truck 51 wins the beauty contest.

From 1926 through the early 1930s, Chicago's small, wood firehouses were dropping in clouds of splinters as new brick and stone edifices were rising—though none were as tarted up as the Seven Painted Ladies built under Big Bill's gaudy regime.

start of World War II, there was money for these investments. Fire insurance requirements had become stiffer together with beefed-up zoning and building codes. A paid professional fire-fighting force well placed to serve the community was at the top of many planners' wish lists. Some of the elegance of earlier firehouses was re-examined to give visual value for money spent.

An example of this elegance is the beautiful six-bay Italianate firehouse built for Engine No. 5 in Cambridge, Massachusetts, back in 1914. This palatial three-story house looks out on Cambridge Street through Roman arches picked out with white stone. The columns that separate the bays extend up past the second floor as pilasters, enclosing arched three-window sets. Beneath each set are carved scenes in white marble panels depicting the history of fire fighting. Above each set are intricate patterns carved into panels fitting the arched enclosure. The third floor has three-window sets with matching arches beneath a brickwork frieze that is just below the building's roof cornice. In the rear of the house, the hose tower rises to a colonnaded tower with eight sides. The effect is one of absolute symmetry in the tasteful decoration. Detailing of this kind would also show up on the seven Chicago houses discussed earlier and would be evident in other large structures as the 1930s approached.

In Kenmore, New York, their fire headquarters is done in Greek Revival style (long popular in general in Upstate New York) beneath a hip roof and using similar stone detailing as Chicago's Painted Ladies. Here, four bays are beneath depressed arches and,

In 1890, Chicago firehouse builders tried to raise the bar a bit architecturally by adding this three window simulated bay with its faux gabled roof that was actually a pediment. By 1926, the ruin was collapsing on itself and was pulled down for a new firehouse under Mayor Bill Thompson's busy regime. *Ken Little Collection*

As American towns grow, larger becomes better

Even as towns moved their firehouses away from the bustle of downtown to give them faster access to main arteries, the stations being planned and built were larger to accommodate the accelerated growth near the end of the 1920s. While large cities were tied to their network of small houses, small-to-mid-size towns and villages were not so constrained. In these communities, the trend was toward a few large stations spotted geographically.

During the last years before the stock market crash of 1929 and subsequent Depression that lasted to the

once again, symmetry is favored to give a look of elegant solidity. Architects with bond money in their pockets were building structures that kept in step with the past styles, because there was little else they could deal with. The requirements of the fire services had not changed—except for the disappearance of horse amenities—since the early paid departments of the 1860s.

Only architectural technology had changed as opposed to the needs of fire fighting. The Empire State Building in New York was climbing above the skyline. In Europe, a new architectural vision was forming at the Bauhaus in Germany. Frank Lloyd Wright's experiments with building materials such as concrete blocks and pre-cast forms were now appearing in gas-station designs let alone commercial and residential projects. But the architects were faced with public buildings funded with public money and the staunch conservatism that went with that combination. Add to that fire chief who were root-bound in nineteenth century traditions and there was little space left for creativity other than with ornament and the pilfering of "acceptable" European stylings.

From locales where "styles" were actually dictated by public ruling, such as California's Spanish restrictions discussed earlier, architects looking to create larger firehouses have been better treated by more free-thinking state and local governments. Farther up the West Coast, Fire Station 14 in Seattle opened in 1926 with a Spanish tile roof, stucco walls, and parapets at the ends of the roof gables wrapped around five equipment bays. The central office and living unit sits above the central bay, giving the ensemble the feel of an "Alamo" look-alike. Today, art deco training towers rise above the firehouse, giving a modern, surreal spin to the original mission concept. Seattle, to its credit, has never been troubled by unity of style among its firehouses. From Classical Revival

TOP LEFT: Chicago's Engine 65 is one of the "Seven Painted Ladies" built in 1929 with funds received from a 1928 bond issue specifically earmarked for new firehouses. "Big Bill" Thompson spared none of the public monies on this design and its somewhat dowdier cousin, the house built for Engine 129. *Ron Mattes Collection.*

LEFT: Engine 129, another one of Chicago's Seven Painted Ladies, bears a strong resemblance to Engine 65 and Engine 45. Unfortunately, the facade's decorative treatment was left off the side walls, revealing the station's basic two-story design with a pretty face bolted on. *Ron Mattes Collection.*

Chicago's Truck 47 resulted from bond issue cash and Mayor Bill Thompson's desire to be known as a civic "builder" when he wasn't marching to Al Capone's tune. Big Bill managed to give jobs to voters while creating this expensive-looking hodge-podge that had one of the first sets of automatic door openers. It opened in 1928 along with six equally gaudy sisters that opened in 1928-29 and remains in action today. *Ron Mattes Collection.*

The best of Chicago's Seven Painted Ladies, Engine 51 survives as a well-proportioned, only mildly eccentric fire-house. The white trim serves to exemplify the building's height. It has a fortress-like solidity that harkens to the Romanesque firehouses of yore. *Ron Mattes Collection.*

to bungalows to Spanish missions, its planners have tended to be architectural gad-flies.

As the 1920s drew to a close, stirrings of new ideas were appearing. While the town fathers of South Orange were enamored with their Norman Revival five-bay firehouse—complete with gargoyles, stained glass, and a 90 foot tower—a short distance away the fire department at Plainfield, New Jersey, was breaking new ground for a new firehouse. Built facing a busy thoroughfare away from city center, this building, outwardly anyway, owes a design debt to the 1914 firehouse at Cambridge, Massachusetts. The Plainfield design has five bays, but two additional bays have been added to its flanks. The five bays are separated by pillars that continue up to become a pilastrade that also encloses the second-floor window sets. A third floor rises above the central unit's cornice with enclosing pilasters of its own. A nod to decoration comes in the form of lantern lights hung on each of the five bay pillars. Though the original plan stipulated swing-open wood doors, the current building with its modern wide-body pumpers and ladder trucks uses the standard roll-ups.

The entire feel of the building is a whole lot of firehouse supported by not much at all. This illusion is caused by the use of steel-reinforced concrete, a new material at the time. A bit of innovation results in a practical as well as a bragging benefit. As of this writing, the Plainfield Fire Headquarters is the largest firehouse on the East Coast with no internal engine-floor supports.

By 1930, projects begun before the Crash of '29, seemed to be signaling the dying gasp of large, decorated firehouses. No one would ever be able to afford such ostentation again. In Los Angeles, the building designed to house Engine No. 27 and Truck No. 9 was completed. It has three bays beneath a Spanish-tiled hip roof and is flanked by trees. Its ornament is in the form of striated brickwork crossing the lower half of the structure beneath the marble band that carries the carved names of the companies. It is a foursquare-quality building of a type that seems on the edge of extinction.

Similar to the Fire Department Headquarters of Plainfield, New Jersey, this ornate cut stone and fancy brickwork structure at Cambridge, Massachusetts, has six bays and would look comfortable alongside a canal in Venice. It was built in 1914. *Ron Mattes Collection.*

An amalgam of 1926 Spanish tiles and training towers from a later year, this five-bay house in Seattle follows the "big house" lead from Eastern cities. *Ron Mattes Collection.*

The Plainfield (New Jersey) Fire Division is housed in this 1927 steel-reinforced concrete firehouse that is one of the largest on the East Coast with seven doors and no internal supports.

It seems that almost everyone at some time in their lives forms a collection. Stamps, coins, Barbie Dolls, and Star Wars figures start the ball rolling and soon there are Jazz records, rare comic books, thimbles, and antique toys. How many homes have the corner etagere staffed with Hummels™ and Precious Moments™ figurines peering out through the glass in ceramic splendor—and growing more valuable with each passing year?

Fire buffs have collected badges, helmets, patches, antique equipment, and even (depending on the available amount of disposable income) a restored fire engine of their own. For those who collect firehouses, since the objects of their search are hardly portable, they have had to settle for photographs, paintings, and other graphic translations—flat images stored in albums, frames, and Carousel slide trays. In 1994, that all changed.

A series of 14 ceramic cast images of the classic firehouses were made available through Lefton's Roadside America and the Danbury Mint. Most are no more than five to six inches high, yet they reveal the key elements of each classic house down to the fire engine peering out the bay door.

The representations designed for Lefton's Roadside America were the work of ceramic artist, David Stravitz.

"What American boy didn't want to be a fireman when he grew up?" asks Stravitz. "Visiting my local firehouse was always a treat for me. I will never forget the great sadness I felt when it was torn down."

Ron Mattes of Mount Prospect, Illinois, has a collection of firehouse photographs numbering upwards of 30,000. Several are reproduced in this book. His collection also includes all 14 of these ceramic firehouses, four of which are shown here.

The town fathers of Kansas City, Missouri, took advantage of a Depression marketplace in 1931 to buck the trend toward simplicity and futuristic designs of the German Bauhaus to create an Italian Renaissance look for Engine No. 31's two-bay firehouse. The ceramic model takes us back to when the house was new in cream-colored stone with a green tile roof and green bay doors fashioned from Oak timbers. A hose tower and large chimney rise from the rear of the

The ceramic interpretation of Engine 31 at Kansas City, Missouri. Kansas City planners said "No" to stripped-down designs; rather, the prototype to this firehouse, done in Italian Renaissance, tried to put a hopeful face on the Great Depression.

building while a picture balcony complete with faux French doors is front and center waiting for some Doge Nobleman to emerge and wave to the crowd below. Architects Madorie and Bihr brought the whole building in for $39,000 and change.

In Georgetown, Colorado, Alpine Hose Company No. 2 was built in 1874 and gives the feeling of a bell and hose tower with a firehouse attached. Actually, that's close to the truth. A wealthy resident who made his bundle in mining told the Georgetown folk if they would build a suitable tower, he would provide the bell. They did and he did, making this firehouse one of the most recognizable classics. Wood framed in white and trimmed in blue with red doors, the model shows off the style and textures even if the "No 2" was painted between the second-story windows on the original and not above the bay door as on the ceramic piece.

These models leap-frog across the European architecture scene favored by the romantic designers who constantly drew from their bag of tricks to bring a cultural face to this public building. In Buffalo, New York, Frederick W. Humble was hardly that when he sold the city on a series of low-budget French chateaus to house some of their residential neighborhood fire apparatus. In 1894, his working palette included red brick, yellow brick, white stone, and stamped iron. Engine 26, another one of his variations on the theme, is discussed elsewhere in this book. His exquisite plans and drawings didn't quite translate into reality, but Engine 28, recreated in glazed ceramic clay, is a beautiful model that outshines what eventually ended up in Buffalo's neighborhoods.

Two approaches to the fortress look are the houses built in Albany, New York, and Charlotte, North Carolina. These models look like they weigh forty pounds each, and that is the effect their architects were striving for. The Romanesque Albany station built for Engine No. 1 is modeled with only one bay instead of two in its real counterpart. But the rough-hewn, two-tone stone look is carried out, held together by the complex planes of the hip roof, dormers, and copper-sheathed turret. Its partner—not in style, but impression—is Engine No. 6 built for Charlotte. Here, the architects took a basic two-story firehouse

RIGHT: One of the most well-proportioned classic firehouses, Engine No. 1 built in 1892 for the Albany (New York) Fire Department appears heavy with the hewn stone walls of its Romanesque fortress. This model represents the single bay version before an additional bay was tacked onto the rear end.

design, then layered on tons of rough stone. The model looks as though it is being ravaged by rock kudzu; it's all facade that looks ready to fall into the street at any moment. Two bracketed awnings shade Roman arch windows and both bays. On the side, a striped ice-cream store awning shades the street entrance, softening the boulder-strewn facade. Local Charlotte rock climbers could consider this firehouse a challenge.

Norwich, Connecticut's, Fire Department Headquarters is a beautiful, classic red-brick fire station. Like the Albany model and those real houses in York, Pennsylvania, and Ann Arbor, Michigan, it is a completely realized building in three dimensions. There is absolutely no doubt as to its function, and that's what makes it a classic design.

Both the Relief firehouse in Mount Holly, New Jersey, built in 1892, and the Union No.1 in Carlisle, Pennsylvania, that opened its doors in 1885 are cut from the same basic design mold and yet the models point up their subtle differences.

They are both Victorian industrial houses with their towers pushed to the front as if by an impatient stage mother. Both have touches of wrought iron and scrollwork from a jig-saw artist, and both feature the big front doors of their later design modification. On the Relief station, the street entrance door at the side of the building has disappeared, but the essentials are there. On the Union house you can see the brick relief pilasters run up both sides, but only one side is revealed on the actual structure. Today, Union No. 1 is a museum with its new fire department building next door, and Relief is still the oldest active volunteer fire company in America. Like their ceramic model coun-

terparts, this pair of classic firehouses are frozen in time for us to enjoy.

In a time when developers are all too quick with their wrecking balls, these buildings, for all their beautiful and quirky architectural eccentricities, are vulnerable. Some have been converted to other uses while keeping their basic concept intact. Others are landfill. The models allow us to appreciate their essence in three dimensions and raise our curiosity about the time when they were built and about the firemen who lived and worked inside their walls.

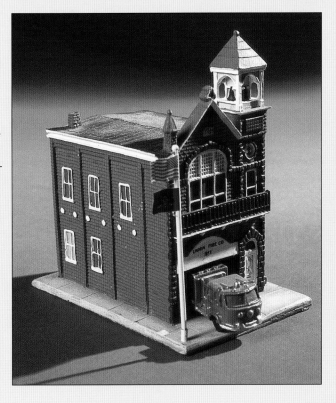

RIGHT: The Union No.1 firehouse built in Carlisle, Pennsylvania, back in 1885 is a classic Victorian industrial structure with its tower pushed to the front; it is delicately trimmed with molded red brick, stained glass, and, for good measure, a bit of ironwork.

FAR RIGHT: In 1874 when the Alpine Hose Company in Colorado built this frame firehouse to support the gift of a fire bell, could they have imagined its ceramic counterpart would grace the shelves of fire buffs across the country 120 years later?

Galena Fire Department headquarters, located just down the street from the original 1851 firehouse, was a WPA project started in 1940 and completed in 1941. Its quarried stone cladding was designed to match the dance hall next door—called a "Turner Hall" by the German-descent population of the period. Parked in front is a 1935 Seagrave Engine.

CHAPTER 6

The 1930s and 1940s: Depression and War Take Their Toll

A GLIMPSE OF THE FIRE-HOUSE FUTURE FOLLOWING THE CRASH OF '29

Changes were on the way as the Depression took hold. Quite a different trend was predicted by two examples of pre-Works Progress Administration (WPA) firehouses, opened years before the WPA was formed in 1935: Engine No. 6 in eclectic Seattle, Washington, that opened in 1931 and the East Orange, New Jersey, Fire Department Headquarters that opened its doors in 1932.

Leave it to Seattle to go for the flash. The firehouse built to accommodate Engine No. 6 reflects two trends that were rippling across America as we stumbled into the 1930s with the Great Depression growing heavier on our backs despite the hot licks of the Jazz Age still ringing in our ears.

It was an era of accomplishment. Lindbergh had flown the Atlantic in 1927. The Empire State Building, the tallest building in the world, was completed. Fast trains were dashing back and forth from coast to coast. Automobiles had become a part of our lives and had graduated from the clunky angles of Ford's Model T to sleeker lines that made them look like they were going fast even when they were parked. Great steamships were coursing between continents as fledgling airlines were reaching toward more reliable and streamlined planes. President Hoover was still promising that the tweak in our financial growth was only temporary and the Volstead Act—Prohibition—had raised alcohol consumption in America to a new high.

The second trend was the way people and city governments now regarded their firemen. The days of the rowdy volunteers were a distant memory. The paid departments and rural volunteers alike were now seen as both skilled technicians and good neighbors.

Seattle's Engine No. 6 literally radiates a new and modern vision. To traditionalists, the firehouse sits in the center of its large lot like the girl who wore a red dress to the wake. Whatever is said about its first impression, Engine No. 6 does not look like a firehouse. But in 1931, that was okay. Pictures in school books and on magazine covers of ultra-streamlined planes and trains didn't look real either. They were a promise—as was Engine No. 6. It foretold of a time when we would not have to look to a rehash or re-interpretation of European styles for our public buildings. Nothing more ever came of this statement by architect George Stewart—thank heavens—but the house is still there, radiation and all.

It is made of solid concrete blocks pre-cast with score marks. The trim is steel. Above the red roll-up bay doors are two glass panels displaying either lightning bolts striking the center flagpole staff that runs up between the bays like a skinny pilaster, or radio waves emanating from some internal source. Take your pick: lightning rod, or radio set. The overall impression is not warm and fuzzy, but stark and technical verging on a metaphor for the skills of the technically proficient firemen waiting within to be called to action.

A painting of General Grant's home—a popular Galena tourist attraction—has been applied to both sides of the hood in the tradition of the decorated hand pumpers of the mid-nineteenth century.

Regarding of the "radio waves" radiating across the front of Seattle's Fire Station No. 6, when it opened in 1932 it did not have any radio communication equipment inside. Architect George Stewart created a nineteenth century station with a "modern" concrete and steel facade. *Ron Mattes Collection*.

The firemen ensconced in Engine No. 6 were, basically, the same fellows who had been fighting fires since the turn of the century. One artifact was gone: The sliding pole, that most unique piece of firehouse furniture, had gone away with the move toward single-story buildings. There would be fewer poles included in future designs, partly because of architectural demands and partly because men were regularly injured using it. Night alarms that brought firemen out of a deep sleep were the primary cause. Hernias, broken ankles, and sprains sidelined many valuable men. Now, living quarters were on the same floor, adjacent to the apparatus bays. The pole would remain and be used until the present in the old houses that remain manned. Tradition dies hard in the fire-fighting business.

Little had changed with their equipment, or "classic" methods of fighting fires. Fire engines were still open-cab affairs. Axes, pike-poles, pry-bars, hose, nozzles—nothing was a great deal different and yet, architects stepping gingerly into the 1930s seemed to want to imbue their firehouses with "modernistic" form. Stewart chose hard surfaces: concrete blocks, polished steel, glass, and linoleum floors inside. Painted steel machines sat inside this blockhouse with a smaller blockhouse bolted alongside.

The good old blue-shirts went about their business probably much like the firefighters of the gingerbread firehouse at Oakland, California, discussed earlier. Inside the striated concrete, they carried on the nineteenth century way of life. This included clinging to the Gamewell-type paper tape and telegraph method of receiving alarm calls. For all its radical radio chic, there was no radio inside.

Another lunge at modernity, the firehouse at East Orange, New Jersey, reaches for more legitimate paternity and less fantasy than Engine No. 6. Architect Frank Bowers Jr. took a page from the Bauhaus school of design founded in Weimar, Germany, back in 1919 by Walter Gropius. According to Gropius, a designer should view each project on the basis of its own needs, without reference to previous forms, and should make use of modern building techniques and construction materials. A look at the Bauhaus school building speaks to Gropius' guiding principles: uncluttered, balancing wall surfaces with window placements and simple forms. The East Orange firehouse is deceptively modern and almost stark in its lack of ornament. It is all planes and balance of horizontal and vertical forms. A planter extends across the three bay doors, acting like a balcony that would have, forty years ago, been made of wrought iron. The hose tower rises at the back of the house in two parts pressed together with one that is vertically striated with brick. Just three touches of blue color are on the front: a molding beneath the house name, an awning over the street entrance, and a single blue circle of terra cotta in the balcony's massive support pillar.

F. A. Gutheim, an architecture critic, wrote in the *American Magazine of Art* in 1933, ". . . The great majority of public buildings have been characterized by a dusty formalism and routine flatulence; our worst architectural failing of all is a sentimental pretentiousness, and in public buildings, this is carried to its extreme point. . ." He goes on to single out a few worthy of praise. "Here and there, almost accidentally, good modern buildings are being built." Making his "A" list is the East Orange Fire Headquarters.

When the WPA went to work in 1935, the Public Works Act leadership realized that not every building

BELOW AND INSET: Built with funds from the Works Progress Administration (WPA) in 1932, this fire headquarters at East Orange, New Jersey, was designed by architect Frank Bowers Jr. It represents a certain basic modern approach in vogue for public buildings during the Great Depression. It escaped the "public flatulence" typical of many WPA projects according to one contemporary critic. Despite the trappings of modern architecture, the interior operation was that of a nineteenth-century firehouse.

created by the make-work projects would be an architectural jewel. After a few projects had been completed, the PWA said, "Although some of the buildings erected by WPA labor are admittedly not of good architectural design, in the main the WPA has had an influence, recognized as good, upon public architecture standards."

Architecture aside, the view of the fireman and fire fighting was undergoing a radical change as we dragged ourselves though the 1930s. Rebecca Zurier, in her wonderful book, THE FIREHOUSE, unearthed a great quote that focuses attention on the fire department as viewed by the folks who paid the freight, the town and city governments.

Thomas F. Dougherty, New York City's fire chief, wrote in 1931:

> "Say 'railroad' to the average American and he immediately conceives a mental picture of a tangible, concrete enterprise involving million of dollars worth of capital and thousands of employees. But say, 'fire department' to the same man and his resulting vision is a soft-focus study of a group of blue-shirted men playing pinochle between occasional orgies of water squirting and ax swinging. . . It is a bit of a shock to discover that the operating costs of the New York Fire Department exceed the costs of any one of forty-two rather important railroads . . . The fire department is Big Business. It is a highly specialized, scientific business combining the fascinating problems of engineering with the intricate tactics of warfare and the complicated organizational problems of Twentieth Century industry."

At about the same time, an overhaul of American fire departments was taking place from within. The firemen began to see themselves as professional technicians and practitioners of the science of fire fighting. Classrooms opened up around the country making courses in building construction and chemistry available to firemen. Where training used to be limited to the physical work of putting water on a fire, of scaling and ventilating a building, now rookies and old timers alike had to learn about new flammable materials such as plastic, celluloid and various chemicals.

A man taking some rest time in the firehouse between calls would as likely be reading a textbook on flammable materials' flash points as he would be playing cards or listening to the radio. Outside the firehouse, he was not alone.

On October 8, 1920, the anniversary of the Great Chicago Fire, President Woodrow Wilson proclaimed National Fire Protection Day. The concept was immediately embraced by towns and cities across the country, and an obscure National Fire Protection Association (NFPA) founded in 1896 suddenly found itself atop of wave of public support. National organizations such as Rotary, Kiwanis, and the Boy Scouts began sponsoring attic clean-out days, fire safety weeks, and campaigns focused on home and business fire prevention.

The NFPA began sending technicians around the country carrying the message of practical fire prevention to schools, businesses, and to the firemen. Once trained, the firemen themselves began speaking at Scout meetings and in classrooms on how young people could take on the responsibility to see that their home was fire safe.

This awareness by the American public and especially by town and city governments had a two-fold effect. The cost per capita for fire loss among tax payers dropped between 1920 and 1928 from $3.81 to $2.70. On the other hand, towns who were struggling with antiquated fire-fighting facilities needed help from wherever they could get it—even the federal government that had let them down.

THE GREAT DEPRESSION AND THE GAMES OF WPA

When the bottom dropped out of our economy, new construction seemed to halt, out of breath and swaying from the post-World War I expansion of home and commercial projects. Suddenly, there was no money in the banks, there was no money to be had from private businesses, and there was blessed little money in the pockets of those who were being dumped onto the streets from their paying jobs. The full effect of the stockmarket crash in 1929 was not felt until 1930–31, but it was hard on cities and disastrous for smaller communities. When a mid-size Midwestern town lost both of its banks within a month of each other, everything ground to a stop. Rural villages could at least feed themselves with gardens and livestock, but the barter system was all that was left for exchange of services. How were towns going to pay their civil servants, teachers, the firemen and police? "Anticipation Warrants" were used in some locales. These pieces of paper carried the face value of the employee's salary and could be used to buy necessities or cashed at currency exchanges—another new industry to appear on the scene once banks had folded. However, the warrants only represented the "anticipation" that there would be cash available to back them up. When the body which issued the warrant got some money, the portion would be passed along to the employee. That was where the "anticipation" came in. Mostly, the warrants were sold by holders for a cash fraction of their face value to speculators or merchants who were in the same boat.

Into this financial quagmire came President Franklin Roosevelt in 1933 with his New Deal, part of which was an alphabet soup of new government agencies: the Public Works Act (PWA), Works Progress Administration (WPA), National Recovery Act (NRA), Civilian Conservation Corp. (CCC), Agricultural Adjustment Act (AAA), and many more. Mayors and town councils across America seized on these Federal programs as means to bring in jobs and to create something substantial that their people could point to as positive steps toward recovery. The planning and construction of a new recreation park, library, or firehouse took men off relief, put tools back in the hands of skilled labor, and provided new income for businesses who supplied the raw materials. Toward this end, architects found a willing, or rather, desperate audience in local government meeting rooms.

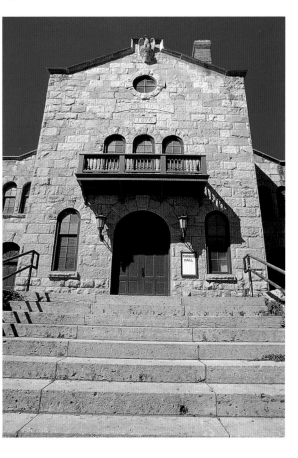

One of these small communities was Galena, Illinois, the town that was supposed to beat out Chicago back in the 1840s when both were rough-and-tumble centers of commerce. Chicago had Lake Michigan and the Chicago River, but up in the northern part of the state, Galena had the Galena River traffic and some very rich lead mines. When the first railroad left Chicago in 1848 for a short run on strap track west to the Des Plaines River and back carrying a few sacks of wheat and a dozen dignitaries, it went by the name of the Galena & Chicago Union Railway. But then the Galena lead mines petered out and Chicago ended up as the railroad hub of the continent. River traffic dropped off.

A failed army officer who worked as a clerk in a Galena leather goods store packed his bags and left town as the Civil War was brewing. Nobody in the riverside community thought old Ulysses S. Grant would ever be worth a hill of beans. And so went Galena's luck.

Galena did hang on and made a middling-size success of itself as a commercial business and farm center. Its 1852 firehouse is described earlier in this book. Five separate fire stations operated in the town starting back in 1830 as the Galena Fire Protection Company. By 1935, the Great Depression had pretty well ground down the town's economy, so it was decided that five fire stations be reorganized into the Galena Fire Department and housed in one centrally located facility. The town is built on a hillside that slopes down to the river's edge, behind a high dike. The new firehouse was sited less than a half block from old Fire Station No. 1 at the corner of Hill and Bench streets. From this overlook above the town, Bench Street allows firefighters to head up or down river. Hill Street is a straight drop into the center of the commercial downtown.

Five years after the reorganization, money finally came to hand through the WPA. Walter H. Cullen, an architectural engineer, was hired and everyone took a hard look at the site. Local stone had been used to build a Turner Hall next to the firehouse site. Now, it wasn't *the* Turner Hall, but *a* Turner Hall. This hall was a community gathering place for lectures, parties, dances, and other social occasions. The Germans called this kind of meeting place a Turner Hall, and several can be found throughout the U.S. in communities rooted to German immigrants. The stone is a beautiful cream color and the hall's architecture is a mix of Roman arch windows and Spanish Mission trim with a red bal-

Inspiration for the new, post-Depression firehouse at Galena, Illinois, was the old Turner Hall building, adjacent to the site of the new firehouse. The City wanted the new firehouse to be built of stone that would match its 1874 neighbor-to-be, shown here in 1997; in fact, the new firehouse would be joined at the hip with Turner Hall to take advantage of the latter's ample heating system. Note the balcony and and roof peak details that would also be reflected in the firehouse design. Searchers took some time to find the same Illinois quarry that produced the stone for this Turner Hall.

Galena's new firehouse is shown nearing completion in 1940. Originally a two-bay house, two more bays—using the same quarried stone from Warren, Illinois—were added later. *Galena/Jo Daviess County Historical Society & Museum Collection.*

This construction-era view of the new Galena firehouse looks past Turnerî Hall (left) toward the WPA firehouse. Note the quarried stone piled up next to the steps. The firehouse heating plant was installed in the dance hall for convenience and space-saving. *Galena/Jo Daviess County Historical Society & Museum Collection.*

cony and matching central arch doorway.

It was decided to build the firehouse of the same stone and follow the same architectural lines. The large heating plant for Turner Hall could also heat the firefighters. So, a pitch was made to the WPA, and the bean counters in Washington didn't bat an eye at funding the first firehouse built to look like a dance hall. After all, it made use of local stone, had no superfluous ornament, and looked like a cheap proposition using the volunteers to help with the finish work.

Then came the matter of the stone. With a small residence removed from the site and the plans approved by the WPA, finding stone that would match the Turner Hall's facade suddenly became a problem. The hills around Galena are carved up into numerous quarries, but which one had the right stone? Walter Cullen was a stone mason as well as architect for the project and he thought he had found the right stone in nearby Horseshoe Mound, but no luck. Over 35 local quarries were examined and their various samples displayed in Mayor Gamber's barbershop window. Finally, someone looked up the old files of the Galena *Daily Gazette* and found a piece on the construction of the Turner Hall dated June 8, 1874. In the article, it was mentioned that stone had arrived from Seda Quarry.

Mayor Gamber wasn't about to lose that WPA money and decreed a statewide search if necessary, ". . . to find that quarry if they had to go all the way to Hong Kong!" Late that afternoon, searchers found a local in Warren, Illinois, some 25 miles east of Galena who led them to an abandoned hole in a hill that had the exact stone they needed. Now all they had to do was lug 400 cubic yards of the stuff back to Galena. Mayor Gamber and his Rock Committee decided it was cheaper to have the stone cut and dressed at the quarry, then hauled to Galena, than to ship the WPA employees to the site. That accomplished, the "dancehall firehouse" was on its way to completion.

Work began on April 20, 1940. First, 2,000 cubic yards of dirt and 845 cubic yards of rock were excavated and hauled away, then they poured almost 200 cubic yards of concrete for the foundation, retaining walls, and first and second floors. The original design called for a two bay house with enough room inside for three trucks and two boats—after all, this was a river community. The plans called for a drying rack for the hose rather than a hose tower.

A 40-foot-square meeting room, a 24 x 20-foot club room, and a 10 x 14-foot kitchen occupy the second floor. Since this is a volunteer house, there is no dormitory and thus no sliding pole. Originally, the city thought several shifts of men could work out of the station, but WPA rules forbid that concept; though the project was a local one, the WPA did control the purse strings. Barbering suffered in Galena during the Mayor's bouts with the government men, but the project went doggedly ahead.

The *Daily Gazette* of November 28, 1940, rhapsodized:

> "When completed, the new firehouse will be a building of which Galena citizens may be proud. Besides being a beautiful addition to the city, it will be a gift to the fire men that they have deserved for many years. It will be a gift in one sense of the word, but on the other hand, many of the local fire men have donated time and work on the project themselves, and too, they have earned far more than the value of their new home.
>
> "It will also be a gift to the tax payers, to be paid for by the tax payers. When a man buys a new car and hires a chauffeur, he usually provides a good place in which to keep his purchase. When the Galena tax payers approved the purchase of new fire equipment they were not forced to hire a fire department. A group of public-spirited men was already organized to take care of the equipment and there is no argument but that the Galena firemen handled the job faultlessly under adverse conditions. So, the new firehouse is not only a gift to the firemen, it is a place where the firemen can take care of the tax payer's equipment."

By May 1941 the firehouse was finished. All it needed was a suitable kick-off, a ceremonial endorsement. An invitation was sent out to the Southern Wisconsin/Northern Illinois Firemen's Association for their 28th annual convention. They accepted, and 500 firemen made plans to converge on Galena. In the bygone days of volunteer conventions, marking out a parade route would have been high on the list of priorities, followed closely by a contract to the local silversmith for some engraved trophies and commemorative silver plate. A grand banquet—or two—would be laid on with a trencherman's board groaning under the weight of four or five entrees plus wines and cigars.

But this was the spring of 1941, and many traditions of the volunteer service had gone away along with most people's money. The attitude of the service had also changed as the new professionalism was also practiced by these part-time firemen. Volunteer training

had improved, and many companies sent their men to train with paid departments and sent them to colleges that offered new courses in fire fighting and fire prevention. As the war in Europe intensified, preparedness was preached from government pulpits. The draft had been reinstated. The manufacture of military goods for Britain and the reinforcement of our own depleted armed forces had added jobs to the economy. News reels of bombed European cities and air raids by the Japanese on China had heightened everyone's awareness that isolation from the conflicts was becoming more difficult.

In this atmosphere of national economic woes and international war, representatives of 38 Wisconsin and Illinois fire departments descended on Galena to meet and to compliment the new firehouse. Although there was celebration and probably some vigorous elbow-bending between sessions of the formal program held in the firehouse meeting room, this was hardly a party-hearty crowd. As the *Daily Gazette* tells us:

> "Appearing on the program will be such men as Richard Widman, Chief of the Madison, Wisconsin, Fire Department; O. A. Glasow, Chief Electrical Inspector, Northern States Power Co.; Richard E. Vernor, Manager, Fire Prevention Department, Western Actuarial Bureau; Roy Alsip, Chief of the Champaign, Illinois, Fire Department; and W. B. Devereaux, Special Agent in Charge of the Federal Bureau of Investigation."

Following their words, a fire college film was shown. To add some luster to the proceedings, the St. Michael's School Band played selections at both morning and evening sessions. With effusive praise and the tooting of a brass band, Galena's new firehouse was officially added to the volunteer ranks.

Two more bays were harmoniously added in 1969

Galena's restored 1935 Seagrave engine in front of the 1940 firehouse. The engine was in use until 1968, was sold, then returned to the department in 1997 for restoration.

This somewhat wall-eyed design was created for the Denver Fire Department by architect Raymond Ervin in 1939 to house Engine No. 9. Built of two colors of common brick, it is a box without any redemption. The symmetry is absolute and it is typical of the architectural void described earlier. This was not a WPA building, but it was ordained by the Federal Emergency Administration of Public Works—an agency of the PWA. It was PWA model No. 1270-F. *Ron Mattes Collection.*

and today, Fire Chief Mike O'Neill heads up a department of 34 volunteer members. The firemen have drill sessions every Monday as well as one meeting per month, followed by a meal cooked in the house kitchen. Potential new members become probation volunteers ("probies") until they have attended as many drills and fires as possible. A written test follows and then the probie is voted on by the entire membership. Through fund raisers, they have bought pagers for the volunteers as well as the latest-design fire helmets. They have also added a Ford 8000 rescue truck complete with a Hurst Tool ("jaws of life") to their apparatus roster. One of their early motorized units, a 1935 Seagrave Engine with a painting of General Grant's house on both sides is currently being restored by the volunteers.

This 1940 firehouse designed to look like its dance hall neighbor is a somewhat unique WPA success story. As with most WPA projects of that time, however, the community and local government worked hard together to provide that "gift" to themselves and their firemen.

Some federally backed firehouses were more successful than others. Often, city sponsors accepted an off-the-rack design that corresponded with the opinion of the architecture critic quoted earlier when he

bemoaned, "...architectural flatulence." Consider firehouse model No. 1270-F funded by the Federal Emergency Administration of Public Works for the citizens of Denver, Colorado, in 1939. This is a two-story box trimmed in two colors of common brick with a wraparound effect around the second floor windows that gives it a wall-eyed aspect. There is absolutely no ornamentation. Architect Raymond Ervin hopefully worked under extreme duress and went on to greater glory. It is a sturdy utilitarian box, attributed to by the fact that it is still in operation today for Denver's Engine No. 9.

WPA firehouses covered a wide range of designs that were definitely not flatulent. Cincinnati was given a real gem in the form of Engine No. 2, created in the Walter Gropius Bauhaus style used for the East Orange house discussed earlier. This 1939 firehouse uses flat planes and striated dark brick courses that stand out in relief for decoration. Rounded interior bay supports break up the flat slabs and relieve the eye. The four bays span the entire building front except for the central street door. Maintained in excellent condition, this firehouse is still in operation and inspires the same admiration as would a restored fire engine of the same period.

Another successful WPA project completed in

A kissing cousin of New Jersey's East Orange Fire Headquarters discussed earlier, this Cincinnati firehouse built for Engine No. 2 in 1939 is an elegant demonstration of what was possible from the WPA. Striations created by using dark brick courses in relief accent its horizontal lines. The rounded interior bay supports break up the flat slabs. *Ron Mattes Collection.*

The ultimate in truncated skyscraper chic, this WPA structure built for Minneapolis in 1940 for Engine 8 is still in operation today. Hiding behind pilasters that resemble tall buildings, its simple two-story design pushes the WPA mandate for minimum ornament. Thankfully, the treatment is also carried down the side walls to give the building a complete look. *Ron Mattes Collection.*

1940 for the firemen of Minneapolis, Minnesota, is a truncated skyscraper built for Engine No. 8. Hiding behind sculpted pilasters resembling tall buildings, this simple two-story, three-bay design pushes the WPA envelope for extra-curricular ornament. The pilaster motif is carried out on the side walls as well giving the building a completely realized look as opposed to the bolted-on super-facade often used in this style of house. Again, it seems that good styling affects longevity since this is still an operating station today.

A return to the "modernism" of the early 1930s gave Engine No. 1 in Indianapolis, Indiana, a retro look in 1938, calling up Art Deco touches with the rounded corner frame around the bays and the steel support pillar that separates them. It substitutes shapes for the lightning bolts scribed into Station No. 6 in Seattle featured in the previous chapter. The corners on the Indianapolis house are rounded with a semi-circular treatment that resembles the tail-end observation car of a streamlined passenger train. This projection is matched to a lesser extent by the office block on the other side. With the hose tower in the

rear looking like a high tail, does anyone else see a symbolic airplane here? Apparently, its train/plane modernism couldn't save it as a firehouse. It was closed in 1982.

If WPA projects existed only as rigid patterns, then this station would never have been approved. But Green Bay, Wisconsin, still enjoys its 1937 residential firehouse. A few dormers, a bit of Greek Revival trim, three depressed arches, and homey double-hung windows allow this building to fit perfectly into its residential site. Its brickwork is excellent, using a subtle two-color treatment—but not laid in simple courses. The whole small-town look is symbolized by the little cupola on top, stuck up there as a nod to tradition when every firehouse was incomplete without its bell tower.

For federally funded agencies, the WPA and PWA managed to leave behind more good firehouses than bad, put a lot of skilled workers back on a payroll, and kept Depression-poor contractors in the black. There was as much innovation as there was "flatulence," and most of these projects would look like fine art compared to what was coming.

This WPA model resembles the ideas behind Station No. 6 built in Seattle back in 1931 featured in Chapter 5. The single-story firehouse combines a rounded corner art-deco frame around the bays whose central support pillar is steel. Rounded corners are used throughout with the firemen's day room jutting into the lawn as a half-circular bay. *Ron Mattes Collection.*

As if to demonstrate that the WPA did have a soft spot and was not above incorporating some dormers, a bit of Greek Revival, a few arches, and homey double-hung windows, the specs for this 1937 firehouse—Engine No. 3—in Green Bay, Wisconsin were approved. It meets all the demands for a residential house in a residential setting, and it remains open today. *Ron Mattes Collection.*

Old Station No. 2 holds a Pierce pumper and a Ford Med-Tech ambulance. Out in front is the Captain's buggy or "command vehicle." The facility was intended to serve a volunteer force when it was under construction in 1956, but by the time it opened in 1957, Arlington Height's first six paid men moved in. Remodeling over the years adapted it for sleeping and meals required of the 24-hours-on/24-hours-off shifts.

CHAPTER 7

Post World War II to the Present: Decline and Technology

FIREHOUSES DECLINE AS TECHNOLOGY IMPROVES

World War II brought everything to a screeching halt. With our entrance into the war against both Japan and Germany, our stunted economy climbed out of the hole dug by the Great Depression and double-timed into a war economy. Defense plants began churning out tanks and guns instead of Fords and washing machines. Travel for the average citizen became almost impossible, with trains committed to troop and war materiel transport to both coasts, airplanes were only for the privileged or the well-connected, and driving the family Dodge down to the corner store for a quart of milk was virtually unpatriotic. Rationing books were issued for food, clothing, tires, gas, and even shoes—so even walking was a poor option.

Fire departments were allowed gas and tires since they were also part of Civil Defense, but they gave up their red and green glass from their flashing lamps to be melted down for lamps in bombers that told parachutists when to jump—and for night-vision lights in submarines. Chrome, copper, stainless steel, and nickel were other casualties. A 1942 advertisement by American La France underlines their patriotic sacrifice:

> "A new color trim to replace the chrome-plate is part of YOUR contribution to insure VIC-TORY. . . One item—nickel—formerly used as the under plating on chrome plate trim on American La France fire fighting apparatus (for 12 months production) is sufficient to properly alloy 50,000 pounds of armor plate. Yes, YOU are insuring [sic] VICTORY when ordering your fire engine in war dress."

One other thing fire departments lost besides their chrome plating was their men. Rosters shrank as firemen signed up for the war effort. They were highly sought after for enlistment since they were physically fit, above average intelligence, and were used to a military teamwork structure; they also had the guts that came from fire fighting. During the war, many fire departments closed firehouses and consolidated operations. Old steam pumpers that had been sitting in the rear of the engine room waiting to be hauled out for parades, were inspected, stoked up, and put into active reserve, usually being towed by a tractor.

The building of new firehouses went into almost complete hiatus until after VJ Day in 1945. The men and women of the armed forces came home to the G.I. Bill, to college educations, to low-cost housing loans, to new cars running on better highways, to a prosperity unmatched in American history. It was here, during this giddy rush for a piece of the American Dream, that the firehouse started into its period of decline.

An explosion of new technology engulfed postwar fire fighting. Plastics, synthetic rubber, self-contained underwater breathing apparatus (SCUBA), walky-talky mobile radios—all the breakthroughs that occurred under the stress of wartime science—found their way into the firehouse. Fire-resistant turn-out coats hung from the pegs, nylon and Dacron fabric added strength and durability to the hose hanging from the drying rack, and in many houses radio speakers now blared out fire locations, replacing the old telegraph system. Fire engines parked in the bays now had enclosed cabs large enough for the whole

Harkening to the fire memorials erected during the period of Victorian adoration of firemen, this life-size monument to Arlington Heights firefighters stands in the middle of the downtown area near the railroad depot. It was modeled after an actual AHFD fireman, complete with gear. *Courtesy Arlington Heights Fire Department.*

crew, and radios in the chief's cars and trucks could keep constant communications flowing. Glass and aluminum roll-up doors replaced the old swing-out portals. The strength of these new doors allowed for larger doorways to accommodate the larger aerial ladder trucks, rescue vehicles, water tankers, pumpers with large booster tanks, and the new "quad" trucks that included aerial ladder, pumper, hose wagon, and water tanker all in one vehicle.

Where could a decline begin with all this technology infusing the war against fire? Its roots were in the 1930s when houses were built like Engine No. 6 in Seattle, and the optimism toward the machine age and city planning was reaching its peak from the mid-1920s. Its roots also lay in the new awareness of fire prevention begun in this same time period. The expansion of cities was postponed by the Depression and then again by the war, but in the 1950s urban flight to the suburbs was in full swing. City planners had to decide how to grow with this explosion—as well as how to protect their swelling populations.

Their solution seemed to lie in both the new technology that allowed greater fire-fighting efficiency

with fewer firemen and also the shift in public opinion about firemen in general. Shortened work weeks inherent in the new three-platoon systems and a drift away from the hero-on-a-pedestal image to ordinary blue collar—or blue shirt—workers weighed heavily on government decisions about their firehouses. City fire departments were unionized into the International Association of Fire Fighters of the AFL-CIO, and suburbs were shifting from volunteer to paid companies. The firehouse became a place to go to work rather than a home away from home. Within the ranks, firefighter spokesmen began lobbying for less money to be spent on firehouse design and amenities and more be set aside for better salaries and shorter hours. Some fire departments had to resort to strikes to raise pay and benefit levels. Firefighter publications dropped columns and features focusing on quaint stories told 'round the potbelly stove in favor of articles on technical subjects and professional concerns.

On another level, many fire departments were accepting responsibility for ambulance services. Although this was not that unusual as far as providing the vehicle and a driver was concerned, the "ser-

The one story, drive-through firehouse built in 1974 in Holland, Michigan, displays modern equipment on the ramp, including from left: a 1990 E-1 pumper, a 1974 Sutphen 1141 Aerial Tower, and an Eagle pumper refurbished from a Sutphen after a wall fell on it. To the right is a community meeting room and offices. On the left is the firefighters' day room and kitchen.

vices" part now included medical training for ambulance attendants. In communities where ambulances had been furnished by the local undertakers, firemen found themselves being required to learn emergency medical techniques to perform at the fire or accident site. A new branch of medical practice was created, the Emergency Medical Service (EMS) and its attendant word, "paramedic." For the first time, firehouses found ambulances sharing their bays alongside pumpers and ladder trucks.

Specialization now includes marine safety and rescue in towns where recreational lakes or access to larger bodies of water pose a possible threat. Holland, Michigan, is a tourist town that shares the west side of Lake Michigan with other similar tourist destinations like Muskegon to the north. Their four-bay drive-through firehouse was built on a coal yard back in 1974. It is a thoroughly modern, architecturally neutral collection of one-story modules. On the entrance side are offices and a public meeting hall that doubles as a classroom for the half volunteer, half paid department. In the center are the four staggered bays and on the far end are the paid-firemen's dormitory, the full kitchen and dining area plus the day room where the engine and ladder truck drivers spend their little free time. What makes the firehouse unique is not its design, but the inflatable Sea-doos and other rescue watercraft that are part of their equipment compliment. Many firehouses have scuba-certified members even if the only body of water is a nearby river. Add one more chore to fire fighting and medical emergencies readily accepted by these professionals and volunteers.

Outside press scrutiny of department operations, budgets, and hiring practices, especially as they concerned minorities, has become more critical. No longer is the fireman held above other city workers in the perception of many government planners. When city budgets and political agendas raise their fiscal and electoral heads, the honeymoon is over.

Every city and village in America handled this period between the 1950s and today's fire departments in a different manner though there were many common threads. For this book, we'll look at Arlington Heights, Illinois, a nationally known suburban village 30 miles northwest of Chicago, and we'll return for the last time to the Windy City on Lake Michigan that was so devastated by the great conflagration of 1871.

Arlington Heights is known nationally and internationally for its race track, the Arlington Park International Raceway, which closed down in 1997 after a

The dormitory room, shared by the full-time members of the Holland Fire Department, is kept neat. Originally a 24-hour department, these Michigan firefighters now work in 12-hour shifts that end at 8 p.m. and 8 a.m.

A modern kitchen and dining area is a well-planned feature of the Holland firehouse. The men chip in for meals and share the cooking and clean-up chores.

Because the Holland firehouse is near a recreational lake, Sea-Doo™ and Whaler™ rescue boats are part of the equipment roster.

spat with the state government in Springfield. The village fire department is another matter. Instead of downsizing or shuttering firehouses, it is adding to the four houses currently operating, and has one of the finest departments in the State.

This building program is a trend among mid-size towns caught in the pattern of suburban growth. Corporate headquarters are leaving the city's high taxes for the wide-open spaces of built-over farm land. A neighbor to the east, Mount Prospect, just finished building a new combination fire and police building next to the Union Pacific Railroad tracks that serve commuters in this northwest corridor to and from Chicago. It is a vast barn of a building with drive-through bays for its engines and ladder trucks.

Their department answers an average of 5,000 calls per year with 60–70 percent of those calls being EMS related.

The Village of Arlington Heights also straddles this three-track commuter and freight railroad. It was the coming of the railroad in 1854 that spurred Arlington Heights' growth when it was a few homes and stores at the intersection of a Native American trail and the single track of the Illinois & Wisconsin Railroad. At that time, the town was named after is founder, William Dunton. A great wave of immigration replaced the Yankee storekeepers with no-nonsense German stock, and the newspaper was printed in two languages.

By the time of the Civil War, there was no fire

The combined fire and police station in Mount Prospect, Illinois, is a take on an old-fashioned red-brick firehouse. It is sited on the edge of Northwest Highway, a busy thoroughfare that parallels the Union Pacific/Metra railroad main line. This larger structure replaced the old fire/police building, but it suffers from the same problem: Evening rush-hour and commuter-pickup traffic often block the exit even though there is a zebra stripe on the street to halt motorists slowing for the nearby traffic light.

department, volunteer or otherwise. Neighbors would just come a-runnin' with their buckets and shovels. On October 9, 1871, friends and neighbors sat on the flat terrace roof of James Dunton's palatial house on State Road and watched the huge, boiling plumes of smoke rise from a phenomenal fire in Chicago that had been burning all night. Nobody saw the need to march to the village hall and demand fire protection for their town that was mostly made of wood and still sat amidst patches of prairie grass as high as a man's head. In 1888, the Dahlberg residence near the railroad tracks burned to the ground despite the best efforts of the make-do bucket brigade.

By 1894, Dunton had become Arlington Heights—a better name created for selling land plots—and former Civil War soldier and then mayor, Charles Sigwalt, convened the town council to create a fire department. Insurance rates were becoming brutal, and the town's population had boomed up to 1,500 souls. They pooled their cash and came up with $650 to buy a secondhand (because no one in their right mind was still building them) Howe hand pumper, 100 feet of rope to tow the thing to the fire ground, and 15 feet of suction hose to draft water from neighborhood cisterns. She was called "Old Faithful." In a two-hour fire fight, the hand pumper could draft up all the water in the immediate area. As one newspaper account stated about a fire at Fred Hue's barn:

FIREHOUSE COOKING
AN EPICUREAN CHALLENGE

Firefighter Tom Van Dokkumburg is shown creating his renowned "Tommy Boy's Firehouse Mustard." Note that the company members are practicing good fire prevention by keeping an extinguisher close by. Left to right: Dave Horn, Tom, Captain David Serrano and Ted Slenk. *Courtesy, Tom Van Dokkumburg, Holland, Michigan Fire Department.*

TOMMY BOY'S FIREHOUSE MUSTARD

4 cups flour
2 cups sugar
1 tsp. salt
2 cups dry mustard
$1/4$ cup poppy seeds
4 cups white vinegar
24 oz. honey

Mix ingredients. Refrigerate for three days. Makes about six 8-ounce jars.

The fireman's love affair with gastronomic creations dates back to the nineteenth century. Since the earliest fire-fighting companies were on call and spent little or no time at the fire station itself, they nevertheless formed a strong social bond among their members. Firemen spent almost as much time planning dances, receptions, and elaborate banquets as they did fighting infernos. Dinners for these celebrations ranged from simple pot-luck casseroles to multi-level entrees. One such menu from December 14, 1899, included the following:

OYSTERS ON THE HALF SHELL
CELERY, OLIVES
LOBSTER CUTLETS, CHICKEN SALAD
STEWED SNAPPER
ROAST TURKEY, CRANBERRY SAUCE
FRESH ROLLS
ICE CREAM, MIXED CAKES
CIGARS

As volunteer fire departments were replaced with paid firefighters, the epicurean delights faded away. A new problem arose—scheduling shifts and providing time for simpler meals. At the beginning of the twentieth century, most paid firemen worked 24-hour shifts seven days a week. Although they were allowed three hours for meals, it was hardly sufficient for quality time with their families. And, if the

fireman was late returning from his break, he was penalized. Because of this, he usually was limited to forking down dry pork chops and lumpy mashed potatoes at a nearby cafe or grill.

When fire companies inaugurated the two-platoon system, firemen worked alternating 12-hour shifts with no time off. Since at least one meal had to be taken at the fire station, a firefighter usually brought his ham sandwich and coffee thermos with him. It wasn't long before the firehouse personnel tired of this limited option and decided to remodel the interior of their stations to include kitchens. This was possible because of another technological innovation—the switch from horse-drawn vehicles to gasoline power plants now left an open space where the stalls had been. What better spot to install a kitchen, complete with stove, sink, and cabinets? And so a new phenomenon was born. Outside of the military, fire departments were probably the only publicly funded organizations in which men cooked for other men on a regular basis.

Nowadays, cooking and cleaning chores are usually rotated. Scheduling mealtime is another problem. If fires could pace themselves so they break out only between the hours of 9 a.m. and 12 noon and 1 p.m. to 5 p.m., the complexities of firehouse meal planning could be cut in half. Since the firefighter's erratic and unpredictable schedule doesn't allow for the nuances of delicately marinated shish kabob or the showmanship of flaming steak Diane, the cook must create a menu that allows for interruptions and reheating. As a result, most dishes are of the hearty meat loaf, chicken, or casserole type. Still, those limitations haven't hampered the firefighter's creativity. In the early days of firehouse cooking during the 1920s, the Worcester, Massachusetts, company was treated to chicken stuffed with hamburger, and beef stew laced with oysters. Today's subtle ethnic cooking tastes must be modified to meet the fireman's high protein and carbohydrate needs (see "Taco Pie" below).

Another consideration is economy. Since there is little food storage space in most kitchens to accommodate the needs of several large appetites, the firemen are forced to shop several times a week. Most people believe that the taxpayer buys the firehouse groceries. Not true. Each firefighter contributes a certain amount of money each week or month, and the cook or cooks are expected to stay within the budget. As Dennis Smith describes in the book FIREHOUSE, a lunchtime meal of "steak a la rouge" (an elaborate name for flank steak boiled in ketchup and water, topped with onions and served on Italian bread), cost each man $1.50. Ten people contributed, and, since the groceries totaled only $14, the remaining dollar was donated to the Firefighters Burn Center of New York City.

The reader may be inspired by the following recipes contributed by firefighter Tom Van Dokkumburg of the Holland, Michigan, Fire Department:

TACO PIE

2 pie crust shells
2 cups corn chips--half in each
1½ lb. hamburger
2 cups sour cream
2 cups shredded cheese
1 package taco seasoning
1 cup water

Preheat oven to 350 degrees. Bake pie crust shell for 25 minutes. Brown ground beef and drain. Add taco seasoning mix and water. Simmer and drain some liquid. Layer each shell with 1 cup corn chips, half of hamburger mixture, 1 cup sour cream, 1 cup shredded cheese. Garnish with lettuce, cut-up tomato, chopped onion, shredded cheese, hot peppers, and favorite salsa.

FIREHOUSE PIGS IN A BLANKET

¼ cup very warm water	1 egg
1 pkg yeast	3½ cups flour
¼ cup shortening	3 lb. breakfast sausage
¾ cup lukewarm milk	salt and pepper
¼ cup sugar	pinch of garlic
1 tsp. salt	6–8 oz. jalapeno peppers

1. Preheat oven to 325 degrees. Mix water with yeast.
2. Add shortening, lukewarm milk, sugar, salt and egg, mixing with a spoon or dough hook
3. Knead for 5 minutes until smooth and elastic. Place in a round, greased bowl and lightly grease top of dough. Cover with damp cloth.
4. Let rise for 1½ hours
5. Punch it down and let rise for another half hour
6. Roll the dough out with a rolling pin. (You may want to sprinkle with a little flour as you roll).
7. Cut dough into long strips about 4 inches wide. A pizza cutter works best.
8. Mix meat, salt, pepper, garlic, and jalapeno peppers in a separate bowl.
9. Spoon enough meat to run along the long edge of dough strip and roll the dough. The "pig" should be about the size of a hot dog. Bake on greased cookie sheet for 35 minutes or until the crust is golden brown.
Tastes great with catsup.

PRIZE-WINNING FIREHOUSE SPAGHETTI
Courtesy Gerald Knust, Elgin, Illinois, Fire Department

1 lb. ground beef
1 lb. Italian sausage (hot or mild)
3–14 oz. cans tomato sauce
3–14 oz. cans diced tomatoes
1 medium to large onion, chopped
1 lb. fresh mushrooms, sliced
1 tablespoon minced garlic
2 tablespoons brown sugar
Italian seasoning and salt to taste

Brown ground beef and sausage in separate pans. Drain off fat. Saute mushrooms and onions. Combine remaining ingredients in large saucepan. Add browned meats, mushroom, and onions. Simmer, stirring often, for about 2 hours. Remove lid and cook until sauce is reduced to desired consistency. Serve over hot spaghetti and enjoy. Serves 8 hungry firefighters.

A number of firehouses across the country have been recycled into restaurants—some featuring "authentic firehouse cooking." But, to get the full flavor of a firehouse meal and its attendant ambiance, perhaps customers should sit down to a flavorful meat loaf, and, just as they are ready to dig in, answer a fire alarm, jump into a fire truck, battle a blaze, and then return to a reheated blue-plate special. Now *that's* authentic.

"... Alderman Hue told the boys to bring their fire engine into his yard and he would keep them supplied with water. They used up all the water in several wells and cisterns, and hauled more in milk cans and Hansing's water tank, while the bucket brigade did valiant service..."

A rivalry developed between local express men, Louie Clark and Fred Binder. At the sound of the fire bell, they would each start for the fire equipment shed with their team of horses. First one there hitched up to Old Faithful and got $2 for his trouble.

The first firehouse meeting room for the volunteers was the second floor over the village hall. The village bought 24 chairs, two tables, oil lamps, and 24 keys. At the meeting to sign up volunteers, only 34 came forward, and the list had to be passed a second time with harsh admonitions to build the roster up to proper strength.

An Illinois state law was passed in 1895 commanding insurance companies pay to local fire departments 2 percent of premiums collected for the purpose of improvements. The village council jumped on this windfall. A horse-hauled hose cart was bought for $105. Then came a horse-hauled hook-and-ladder truck with wooden fire buckets hanging beneath the ladders. Eventually these buckets broke. After carefully assessing the situation, rubber buckets were purchased. All these antiques were housed in a wooden barn—the first firehouse—on the south side of the railroad tracks. By 1895, Arlington Heights had a fire department equal to any fire-fighting department you could name—back in 1855.

One other memorable occurrence that year was the Diamond Sewing Machine Foundry fire. The town's largest industry burned to rubble for lack of water to fight the fire.

RIGHT: "Old Faithful," the horse-drawn hand pumper purchased by Arlington Heights in 1894 as its sole fire engine. The barrel was filled from cisterns or wells by a suction line, then the hose could put a stream on the fire. The hand pumper could empty all the wells and cisterns in the area of the blaze. *Courtesy Arlington Heights Fire Department.*

TOP: Arlington Heights' first firehouse with the 1894 volunteer fire department standing in front of their ladder truck, hose cart, and Old Faithful. When the waterworks was created, its pumps were also located here.*Courtesy Arlington Heights Fire Department.*

LEFT: In 1895, new uniforms were purchased for the Arlington Heights Fire Department. They were so popular with the men, an ordinance had to be filed to keep them from wearing the outfits all the time; they were intended mainly for parades and special ceremonies. *Courtesy Arlington Heights Fire Department.*

In 1901, the village proposed buying snappy new uniforms for the volunteers for $178 and to drill its first well to provide village-wide water mains. Everybody voted for the uniforms and turned down the water mains. From a slush fund, some money was ponied up to drill one long water main from the well. When people saw they could draw water from inside the house, everybody wanted it. By 1905, with the waterworks set up in the same barn that held the fire equipment, a second hose cart was moved into the barn of one L. G. Helm for fires that might occur on the north side of the railroad tracks. This north-south division of fire-fighting facilities would continue into the present.

In 1917, the first real red-brick firehouse was tacked onto the back of the new village hall. After years of lumbering down rutted streets and farm roads, Old Faithful was pretty worn out. A public subscription brought in $900 in hard cash for a chemical pumper from Peter Pirsch in Kenosha, Wisconsin. A hook-and-ladder truck—also gas-powered—was bought in 1922 for $661.28. After their purchase in 1928 of a Seagrave 600-gallon-per-minute pumper/ladder truck, the Arlington Heights Fire Department barely financed its expenses through the Depression. Part of their ability to spend any money at all when everyone else was flat broke came from a village hall deal cut with the Chicago mob to kick back a percentage of the take from illegal punch boards and slot machines set up in local establishments during Arlington Park's racing schedule. It was the Depression, and they did what you had to do. The *Arlington Heights Herald* ran a headline when pointing fingers from that Big City to the Southeast became annoying: "Arlington Heights is Guilty! So What!"

After World War II, the volunteer fire department was still operating out of the Village Hall Firehouse on the south side of the railroad tracks with their aged pre-Depression equipment (except for a 1937 General quad truck/pumper). The volunteers received $1 for every fire they attended, but if it was a false alarm, they got nothing. In later years, this honorarium was jacked up to $2 then to $3 while the chief took home a five-spot. A fire siren called the men to duty. It would blow, they would grab their helmets and turn-outs, and call the station to find out the fire's location. Designated men made for the firehouse to drive the engines and trucks.

Residential building in Arlington Heights had boomed through the late 1940s and early 1950s as the returning GIs took advantage of Veterans Hous-

ing Administration loans. The one firehouse on the south side of the tracks didn't seem adequate. A long freight passing through town could delay firefighters answering any north-side call. In 1955, the State Fire Inspection Bureau dictated an additional house and a shift to a paid department. Two years later, in 1957, a new house, built for the volunteers, was opened on North Arlington Heights Road. This was a minimalist construction project by local architect Walter Kroeber, assisted by two volunteer firemen as general contractors. It is distinctly residential, with a gabled roof hovering over a low, two-story design

David Mills Jr., a retired Arlington Heights firefighter, was one of the first four paid men assigned to this volunteer house after it opened. "There was a meeting room, a couple of toilets, a place to hang coats, and a kitchen," he remembers. "By the time it

was completed, the volunteers had begun the shift to a full-time paid department. Over the years, it's been remodeled to handle paid men, but when it opened there was no place to sleep."

The paid firemen worked 24 hours on and 24 hours off at this station.

As with fire departments across the country, though the postwar economy was booming, city governments were pulling in their horns and adopting austerity pro-

The original 1928 Seagrave pumper/ladder truck has been fully restored by the Arlington Heights Fire Department for parades and display. *Courtesy Arlington Heights Fire Department.*

grams for public services—at least that's the face the voters saw. Suburban villages like Arlington Heights were annexing neighboring communities and increasing the responsibility for providing fire and police services. New firehouses had to be added to keep up with this growth, but the days of the architectural monument to the brave firefighter were long past.

The old village hall and firehouse were pulled down in 1960, and a new, modern village hall was built. The original plans called for a two-story, three-bay firehouse to be attached at the rear of the building. Village Manager Leonard Hanson had a bad feeling about asking voters to pass a bond issue that included a village hall and a spacious firehouse. Joseph Bennett, the local architect, solved the problem by lopping off both the second story and one bay of the firehouse. When the house opened in 1963, the firemen were stowed in two big rooms alongside the bays—one for sleeping and the other with a kitchen and offices. The work shop is the size of a closet, so the quarters offer the men no place to go when they are on duty.

Five years later, Station No. 3 opened on South Arlington Heights Road, a two-bay house that fol-

One of the original six paid firemen hired in 1957, David Mills Jr. works as a training officer with two recruits. He eventually rose to deputy chief of the department, retiring in 1989. *Courtesy Arlington Heights Fire Department.*

Station No. 3 at Arlington Heights is a no-nonsense austerity firehouse opened in 1968. Two of the three bays are drive-through, but the third was a later add-on due to lack of space in the original design. Simple, pre-fab window-wall panels give an industrial look while saving the village budget.

lowed an architectural pattern that was being repeated across the country. The design is, you might say, "Industrial Park Modern"—standard off-the-rack window/wall exterior extrusions are ranked across the front of the office area and down the living and meeting space. The drive-through bays are clad in dark red brick. Only two of the bays are actual drive-throughs; a third bay was added later due to the lack of interior size to accommodate modern equipment.

In 1971, the last firehouse, Station No. 4, was designed by Bennett within the available budgeted dollars for drive-through two-bay operation. It is also a cramped affair following the design of Station No. 3. A Pierce 1500 pumper and a Ford ambulance comprise the active roster with a 1977 Mack pumper in reserve. As with Station No. 3, its design had to be expanded in 1987 with one more bay that now houses the "Hazmat" (hazardous materials) squad vehicle.

The austerity of its firehouses aside, the Arlington Heights Fire Department is considered to be one of the finest in the state. In 1973, it opened its Fire Academy, passing recruits from two neighboring communities through training. As of 1994, the 100th anniversary of the department, 100 communities comprising over 3,000 men and women had received their fire-fighting training at this facility. In 1997, the Insurance Services Organization (ISO) rated Arlington Heights Number 1—the highest possible rating—in public safety capabilities.

A fifth firehouse has been approved to take over the load from old Station No. 2, the volunteer station that opened in 1957. This new two-story firehouse will cost an estimated $4.6 million dollars and will accommodate the fire department headquarters that currently shares space with the police in the village hall; also added to the package approved by the village council was a fourth ambulance. As with virtually all fire departments across the country, in Illinois, paramedic and village ambulance services have been delegated to the fire department. Each of the three ambulances currently serving the community logged an average of 1,632 calls in 1997. To man this new vehicle, a fourth ambulance company will also be formed. Emergency Medical Training (EMT) in Illinois started in Arlington Heights back in 1972. The AHFD then taught other departments.

ABOVE: The village hall of Arlington Heights attached a firehouse onto the back of the building in 1963. To save money, one bay was lopped off as was the second story for firemen dormitory space. Now, the crews reside in two big rooms that are part of the hall complex next door to the bays.

Growth in light industry and the makeup of trains passing through the village downtown area prompted purchase of an International Hackney Hazmat vehicle and the training of a hazardous materials response team. Arlington Heights is also growing vertically now, as high rise condominium/commercial complexes are raising up around the downtown area. A 100-foot aerial tower was added in 1993 as the high-rise building began.

To cover large fires, neighboring communities have banded together in Mutual Aid groups. Arlington Heights, Mount Prospect, Elk Grove Village, and Des Plaines have formed CCERT—the Combined Community Emergency Response Team. Arlington Heights has emptied its firehouses and called on help

for the largest fire in the modern history of the department when the Arlington Park Race track burned down in 1985 and also when a large fire consumed buildings on Vail Street in the downtown area.

After a very slow start back in 1894, the Arlington Heights Fire Department is now listed among the top 26 fire departments in America. To commemorate its firefighters, a bronze statue of a fireman holding a child was erected in a landscaped court in the center of town. This esteem will be reflected in the new firehouse design that will reflect, ". . . aesthetic design consideration to blend it into the residential community where it is being built," said Deputy Chief Charles Kramer. "Our community and our

A class of firefighters attend school at the Arlington Heights Fire Academy. Begun in 1973, over 100 communities in Illinois have sent their firemen through this program. *Courtesy Arlington Heights Fire Department.*

firefighters deserve the best."

It seems that as the 1950s dictated a new austerity in fire-fighting facilities that has carried through until today, the diversion of funds from creating exceptional or even adequate architecture has been well spent on the men's training and their equipment. As pointed out earlier by a chief of New York City's fire department, fire fighting is big business and is funded with public money. That 100-foot aerial tower, bought in 1993, cost $548,000. The Hazmat Squad vehicle, used for handling hazardous materials, cost

$92,000—and those were 1992 dollars. New technology such as hand-held, or helmet-mounted video cameras that help firemen see through heavy smoke are being purchased by even mid-size suburban departments. At $20,000 each, they strain purses, but as one firefighter put it. "If that was your five-year-old hiding behind her bed in a smoke-filled room, would you think $20,000 was too much?"

Of course, not every city and town bent their firehouse architecture to meet the austerity trend. There are always those fearless communities that want to be

A firefighting class advances a line into the burn tower of the Arlington Heights Fire Academy while another team prepares to work on ventilation through the roof; a pumper purchased for training purposes stands by. Over 3,000 firefighters have taken these courses. The academy is one of a handful in the State of Illinois. *Courtesy Arlington Heights Fire Department.*

Mutual aid was not limited to the Chicago Fire of 1871. When the Arlington Park Race Track burned to the ground on July 31, 1985, units from 24 suburban fire departments eventually were thrown into the battle. Shown Here are a Rolling Meadows aerial tower and a 1968 American La France Spartan Pumper. *Courtesy* Arlington Heights Daily Herald.

avante garde, or at least a cut above the surrounding hum-drum. The pursuit of notable firehouse architecture is kept interesting by these exceptions.

Novelty can always be found in firehouse designs, but the Tucson (Arizona) Fire Department must be congratulated for originality when it approved this design for Station No. 10, opened in 1965. A super-graphic numeral "10" identifies the building with the help of creative typography that creates a double-vision effect when the sun is just right. A bunker-like wall shields the office block from the pointing fingers of architecture critics and fire buffs, but the object of

their barely contained hysteria as they elbow each other aside to photograph this gem are the big red doors. While everyone else in North America switched from swing-out to roll-up doors, the architect of this courageous vision chose solid red panels that slide up into frames above the bays. There, they wait, poised like the blades of guillotines, as the equipment rushes out onto Ajo Way. But, if it weren't for the license of artistic expression, how dull our lives would be.

Another creative vision is the two-bay firehouse built for Engine 32 that opened in 1985 on North

30th Street in Milwaukee, Wisconsin. Here, the architect has taken the elements of the 1890s Victorian firehouse—the thrust-forward hose tower and the scrollwork on the imitation gabled roof peak—and turned them into flat-plane symbols. Red brick, once the staple of industrial-style firehouses, has given way to red tile, and what appears to be white brick quoins running up the sides of the main building and the tower are actually white anodized extrusions. The entire building is a symbolic representation of a firehouse. The greatest departure and the saving grace of the idea is the mural of 1890s fire apparatus executed along the building's street side. If you failed to get the symbolism of the facade, this artwork pounds the lesson home. One is reminded of some of those utility-grade firehouses that spent all their money on the front that faced the street while taking a bare bones approach to the side walls.

Everybody who lived through the fashion horrors of the 1970s remembers the colors that they have long ago weeded from their closets and sent off in the Good Will truck. With a firehouse, escaping those harvest gold and avocado memories isn't as easy. Firehouse expert and tireless photographer George Prop-

Three departments responded to this blaze on Vail Street in downtown Arlington Heights as part of a north suburban mutual-aid arrangement. Shown here is a snorkel unit from Rolling Meadows, an Arlington Heights Mack pumper, and a ladder truck from another northwest suburban Chicago suburb, Buffalo Grove. *Courtesy Arlington Heights Daily Herald.*

Engine 10 in Tuscon, Arizona, opened in 1965 complete with doors that rolled up into the frames above them, waiting like red guillotines for the apparatus to return. *Ron Mattes Collection.*

Engine 32 in Milwaukee, Wisconsin, opened in 1985. Its facade elements symbolize Victorian firehouses of the 1890s by using flat planes and surfaces. The mural on the side of the building relieves its two-dimensionality aspect. *Ron Mattes Collection.*

er found Station No. 3 in Elmira, New York, in all its 1970s grandeur. It is a good-looking building, but the super-graphic colors that gave the Tequila Sunrise drink its name that snake across the doors and end like a pointing finger at the huge numeral 3 bring back memories of Nehru jackets, bell-bottom pants, thick sideburns, and Cuban-heel boots with zippers. The color scheme is the big medallion on a chain hanging across an otherwise nice piece of architecture.

The Engine No. 3 firehouse in Greeley, Colorado, that opened in 1972 deserves an award for the maximum use of textures. At least eight exterior touches and seven complex planes are used in a single-story station. Taken overall, it's a not a bad structural design for what must be a volunteer firehouse. But you have to wonder if pink limestone, redwood beams, and stained glass were available when it was built, would they have been included as well?

The house that holds the all-time record for sheer whimsy is the one built for Engine No. 1 in Parker, Colorado. To describe this firehouse, you feel like you're kicking a kitten, but somebody saw the plans and somebody laid out the money that ate into the Parker fire safety budget. Starting at the top, its tower sports a "widow's walk" similar to those found on whalers' homes on Nantucket Island. From there, you come down to the mansard roof to the elongated Edsel grille or screaming mouth tower. To the left, beneath a continuation of the mansard roof supported by white brackets, are three bays done in homage to the Roman arch. In the center of each roll-up door are super-graphic numbers done in "Old West" typography suggesting a Bob Evans restaurant. To the right are the offices echoing, on a smaller scale, the arched bays. To the undying credit of the Parker town fathers, firemen were not forced to use this firehouse. It was never opened.

While seemingly caught between the austerity trend and the need to stand out, the fire department of Bedford Park, Illinois, opted for a show of steel girders and glass between windowless bunker walls to house Engine Company No. 1. This house on South Archer Avenue, near Chicago's Midway Airport, opened in 1978 and uses the full view of the steel and glass machines inside as part of its architectural statement. It mirrors the feel of flight with its transparent glass walls seeming to support the weight of the steel roof. It is an apt metaphor for a firehouse located next to an airport.

And so we come back to the Windy City 127 years after the Great Fire to pay a closing visit. The Chicago Fire Department (CFD) evolved from the Fire Bucket

Ordinance of 1835 that required a leather bucket for every fireplace or stove and a La Salle Street shed containing two hand-pumper engines and a pine cistern large enough to hold two hogsheads of water. From there it has grown to a roster of over 4,400 firemen and more than 600 paramedics. Their firehouses are scattered all over the city, embracing a wide variety of architectural treatments. Most of them are old and some date back to the nineteenth century. Curiously, the last firehouse that sent out a steam pumper to fight the Chicago Fire in 1871—Engine 17, the *R. A. Williams*—was pulled down in October 1979. That was the same year the Chicago Fire Department built its last firehouse, Engine 112.

As Chicago worked its way through the Great Depression, the wartime, and postwar years, it annexed communities to the north, south, and west,

adding their firehouses and companies to the CFD roster. Throughout the 1920s and 1930s, modern equipment made many of the single-bay wooden houses obsolete, and these were pulled down or sold off. Fewer firehouses with faster, more efficient fire engines, ladder trucks, and the new rescue squads could handle greater areas of responsibility.

After Mayor Bill Thompson's building spree from 1927 to 1929, the Depression shut down most firehouse construction and equipment acquisition. Brick and stone two-story, single- and double-bay firehouses built in the 1880s and '90s were all adapted to the new Ahrens-Fox, Pirsch, and Seagrave equipment.

In the late 1930s and after the war, new closed-cab fire engines and trucks were being offered. These at least provided shelter for the drivers and one passenger, though the rest of the crew rode in the ele-

This home for Engine 3 at Greeley, Colorado, is a mixed media of ski lodge construction utilizing quarried stone, painted red brick, and stressed wood. A "with it" child of the Seventies. *Ron Mattes Collection.*

Super graphics and an Edsel grill treatment on this disaster at Parker, Colorado, couldn't save it. Thankfully, the house was never used—at least not for anything as dignified as fire fighting. *Ron Mattes Collection.*

ments—including the poor tiller men responsible for getting the rear end of the ladder truck around the corner.

This demand for new and multi-purpose equipment plus strained public service budgets coping with postwar expansion of cities and towns caused a drastic downsizing of fire departments across the country. Chicago was no different. In some cases with annexations, when fire stations were located only a mile apart, one would be shut down. The kiss of death would be having a firehouse with two pumpers assigned. Sooner or later, one of them got the boot.

Realizing that firemen would have more responsibilities to cover the smaller companies, the CFD persuaded the city council to allocate $2.5 million to build a Fire Academy for CFD personnel. Its address is on DeKoven Street—on the spot where the Great Chicago Fire started as Peg Leg Sullivan ran out of that burning barn.

The Chicago Fire Department, though tradition-bound in many aspects of its operations due to conservative leadership, did find time to innovate. In 1958, the department created the Bureau of Fire

Investigation. Prior to its creation, many fires in Chicago had started from undetermined sources. The investigators learned to locate not only the point of origin, but the probable cause of fires—an effective method to improve fire prevention.

In that same year, Fire Commissioner Robert Quinn saw a Pitman boom with a "cherry picker" basket attached. He called Illinois FWD Truck & Equipment—the Illinois Pitman dealer—and asked if he could get one adapted to get water up to the basket. To test the idea, he went back to Chicago and hooked up a Department of Forestry truck and boom used for trimming trees, but with a hose line strapped to the boom, and Chicago had its very first test snorkel in service on October 14, 1958. Eventually there were seven snorkel units of this temporary design. This equipment would evolve into Chicago's signature fire-fighting innovation. Quinn accepted credit for the concept—and thereafter became known as "Snorkel Bob." The first true Pitman Snorkel Aerial Tower built on a Pierce truck frame was delivered to Bedford Park on March 31, 1960.

From the time Quinn became commissioner, he pushed hard to raise the bar for higher efficiency. One of his contributions was a building program that lasted from 1958 to 1978 that created 32 new firehouses and major additions. These were quality houses of different designs—mostly boxes—depending on the size of the lot and the station's roster. Where there was sufficient land, a one-story house would be built; otherwise 2–3-story houses were fit into smaller lots. Most of these stations accommodated 70–80-foot ladder trucks of the 1940s and 1950s. With the new trucks and aerial ladders of the 1980s and 1990s measuring around 30 feet in length, an ambulance and a pumper could fit into a single-bay house and four units could fit in an older house built for two trucks. With reductions in the number of men needed for each piece of apparatus and using the platoon system of shift scheduling, overcrowding was minimized in the living quarters.

Nor was there a paramedic in the department when Quinn came in. Only 16 ambulances were operated by the fire department in 1958—and then only as transportation to the hospital. By 1991, 58 ambulances were in service. Quinn had one blind

Steel girders suspending glass-curtain walls between rough brick book-ends marks this Bedford Park, Illinois, home of Engine 1 as an industrial, lighter-than-air structure that fits right into its location in an industrial complex next to Chicago's Midway Airport. *Ron Mattes Collection.*

TRADING ON THEIR GOOD NAME

In Plainfield, New Jersey, you can walk by one of the public schools as classes let out and hear two kids trying to spike a bargain.

"I'll trade you two Firefighter Nelsons for One Captain Chandler."

"No way. You got a Captain Allen? I'll trade you even for him."

"How about two Firefighter Nelsons and one Timothy Lowe Sr.? He's a firefighter and an Emergency Services Technician!"

"Well . . ."

This trading-card craze is part of the Plainfield Fire Department public relations effort so people can get to know their firefighters. Normally the realm of sports figures, Super Heroes, and dinosaurs, these cards have achieved value among Plainfield's school kids.

The only way they can get cards is when the firefighters come to the school to teach about fire safety or when the kids visit the firehouse.

"The cards went over very big when they were first made available," says Captain Platoon Commander, Albert Chandler Jr. "About 70 firemen have cards and we printed up another 25–30 for new firemen. The fact that they're still in circulation and the kids do come to the firehouse looking for specific cards so they could get the whole series makes us feel good and that the cards are doing the job."

Each card has a brief biography of the firefighter and includes a "personal message" to collectors dealing with fire safety.

"It's nice to show up at a school and the kids already know your name," said another firefighter.

"They'll listen to you when they know something about you all ready."

Two firemen work on the hose connection of a 1921 Ahrens-Fox pumper at Chicago's Engine 22 in 1940. These vintage engines would have to last through World War II since fire-engine production was virtually stopped for the duration. *Ken Little Collection.*

A shop spare pumper poses in front of Chicago's Engine 24 house. This photo, made in 1971, shows the 1953 Pirsch with an enclosed cab. The trend to enclosed cabs for firefighters got well under way in the early 1950s. *Photo by Freeman, Bob Freeman Collection.*

side toward the ambulance service. When the new truck or van-style EMS vehicles were proposed over the long, low Cadillac ambulances then in use, he hated the boxy vans. He said, in effect, if he was going to meet his maker, he'd rather do it in style—in a Cadillac. While building up the ambulance force, he started downsizing the number of engine companies. When he came in, there 121 companies, today there are about 100.

Prior to the infamous 1968 Democratic Convention, Mayor Richard J. Daley thought to build a "foreground" fire station, an innovative design that would be showcased during that highly visible summer. He had Engine 42 built. This $700,000 firehouse was ballyhooed in the press and was dedicated with typical Daley panoply. His flacks made sure everyone knew the specs. The house had central air-conditioning, marble-lined showers, and, Hizzoner claimed, ". . . sleeping quarters good enough for Army officers." At the dedication, he regaled the audience with stories of how he visited the firehouse in his neighborhood—the back of the Stock Yards where the poor Irish lived—to talk to the firemen and pet the horses. He beamed as how this was now the largest working neighborhood firehouse in the nation. Above him, "Daley's Pride" brooded from

The original Pitman Aerial Tower designed from Chicago Fire Commissioner Robert Quinn's basic idea of a boom-equipped truck. The very first model was delivered to Bedford Park, Illinois, an industrial suburb south of Chicago, on March 31, 1960. *Courtesy Bedford Park Fire Department.*

This view shows the three original snorkels equipped with hose lines running up to the baskets. The concept of having a boom carry the hose to high elevations was the brainchild of Fire Commissioner Robert Quinn of the Chicago Fire Department after he saw a Pitman "cherry picker" boom and basket in action trimming trees. Quinn ordered one built on a 1958 GMC truck, using a Pitman 50-foot boom. Quinn took credit for the concept and became known as "Snorkel Bob." *Courtesy Chicago Fire Department.*

behind the belt of precast windows that wrap around its blockhouse-like overhang. It was not an architectural success. Today, two of the six bays are used as parking lots for fire officials' cars.

In 1977, architect Jerome Butler designed Chicago's Engine 112 that was opened in 1979. After the war, anonymity became the catch term for public buildings. Slabs, hard surfaces, flat roofs, minimum widow area, and a low-brow interpretation of master architect Mies Van der Roh's dictum, "Less is More." In this case, less was . . . less. Inside, this was a tri-

level building with the dormitory on one level and the offices and kitchen on another—both within one flight of stairs of the apparatus floor. The watch officer and the "joker stand"—radio and alarm equipment—are sealed in a glass cell atop a flight of stairs overlooking the equipment bays. There is ample room for the pumper, a ladder truck, and the command van. All of Quinn's stations were made oversize so as the department grew, there would be room to shift and add equipment.

Of all the Chicago firehouses, the most beautiful is

Chicago's Snorkel Squad 1, in January of 1993, drops its stream on a Monroe Street truck garage. A boom arrangement allows for a more accurate hit on flames. *Tom McCarthy.*

Chicago's Engine No. 112 was the last firehouse built since 1979. It could be sitting on any suburban street in the country. The no-frills trend in a small-to-medium-size American communities extends into major cities like Chicago. This is a public building no different than the offices where you go to get your driver's license. *Ron Mattes Collection.*

Engine 127, opened in 1991. It is, unfortunately, built on land belonging to Midway Airport that is owned by the Chicago Board of Education, so it is only a token CFD firehouse. Engine 127 has eight bays, four leading out onto 63rd Street and four that open onto the airport. The street bays are for the chief, an engine, and an ambulance; from the rear doors emerge an assortment of crash trucks and other specialized vehicles that rush to any aircraft in distress. The building uses alternate-colored brick courses and steel trim—especially around the low tower—in a way that suggests Frank Lloyd Wright's famous S. C. Johnson complex and tower in Wisconsin. The emergency yellow girder pylons separating three of the bays are perfect accents of color. This

firehouse seems to have grown out of the ground and is about as far from anonymity as you can get.

Conclusion

Architecturally, with Engine 127, this book ends on note of hope. Even though we've had some fun with the firehouses that went against the trend of anonymity begun in the 1950s and are still with us, we do appreciate CFD's attempt to create an interesting and functional building. It is too much to ask for a return to the days when a firehouse looked like a firehouse. They are no longer considered challenging commissions for architects since public purses make for rigid restraints and these "glorified garages" cannot be built in expensive bunches like Big Bill

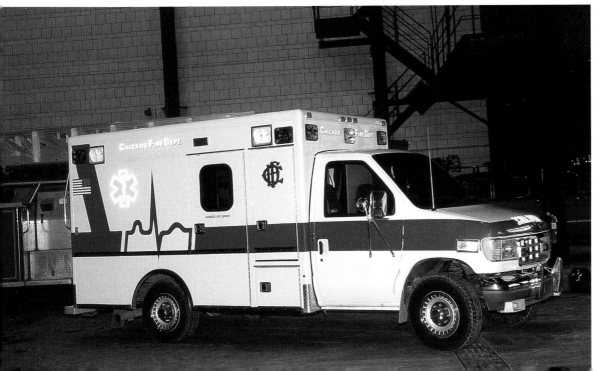

Chicago Engine 98—a Luverne—poses in front of its firehouse near the old Water Works on the city's near north side. The Water Works was the only surviving building in downtown Chicago following The Great Fire of 1871. Engine 98 firehouse, here decorated for the holidays, was built in 1902. *Tom McCarthy.*

A new Chicago Fire Department van ambulance—a Ford Wheeled Coach—represents the increased emphasis on emergency medical services capabilities now provided by most fire departments. *Tom McCarthy.*

Chicago's Engine 42 hunkers down on Illinois Street like a wounded mother ship. In 1968, this state-of-the-art firehouse was Mayor Richard J. Daley's showpiece before the Democratic Convention. Six bays allow it to send forth a dazzling array of fire-fighting apparatus. The interior appointments included amenities any firefighter would appreciate. *Ron Mattes Collection.*

Though officially designated Chicago Fire Department Engine No. 127, the building was constructed on Midway Airport property. Opened in 1991, it is a beautiful building, recalling Frank Lloyd Wright's S. C. Johnson & Son tower and building complex in Wisconsin. Its striped brick courses, use of the round hose tower with steel trim, and the Emergency Yellow bay trim make it a stand-out example of architecture as a modern-day firehouse. *Ron Mattes Collection.*

Thompson's Seven Painted Ladies. Maybe this is rightly so. Where money is spent on embellishment, it is lost for new equipment for fire fighting and survival, better training, and better pay. But when the city planners decide on simplicity of form, the men and women who man these truly unique structures should also be part of the equation.

They are more than public servants. Too often, we only think of them when one or more of their number dies in a fire. Regardless of the growth of EMS calls, there are still fires to be fought. According to *Firehouse Magazine*, there's a structure fire every 55 seconds and a residential fire every 74 seconds—and they are all different. We watch the evening news as the purple-draped engine bearing a firefighter's coffin rolls slowly past, behind the band of pipers and leading the firemen ranked in their dress blues, white gloved hands swinging slowly at their sides. Direct

the architects and the city planners and the dispensers of public coin to stand curbside as one of these processions passes and then go back to their meetings and their drawing boards.

Although the time has come when public buildings have been reduced to block houses and windowless shapes, the fire service deserves better treatment. While brick and stone symbols of 200 years of tradition are a drain on the coffers, the good feeling every community in America has toward our firefighters is worth a second look. They don't need a temple or a pedestal, just a comfortable place to work, to live, and to train for those calls that will test them.

Whether they are volunteers or paid firefighters working a 24-hour shift, wherever they are when they scramble up into that cab in their turnouts should reflect their community's esteem for what they do. Most of the time, that's the only way we can say thank you.

Chicago mourns its fallen firefighters. The Emerald Society Pipe Band leads a procession of firemen in their dress blues and the purple-draped Engine carrying the coffin of a departed comrade. *Tom McCarthy*.

Bibliography

Bales, Richard F. "Did the Cow Do It?" *Illinois Historical Journal*, Vol. 90/ No. 1; Spring, 1997

Braden, Donna R. Leisure and Entertainment in America. Dearborn, Michigan: Henry Ford Museum & Greenfield Village, 1988

Burgess-Wise, David. Fire Engines and Fire-Fighting. Norwalk, Connecticut: Longmeadow Press, 1977

Cromie, Robert. The Great Chicago Fire. Nashville, Tennessee: Rutledge Hill Press, 1994.

Dean, Anabel. Fire! How Do They Fight It? Philadelphia, Pennsylvania: Westminster Press, 1978.

Delsohn, Steve. The Fire Inside. New York: Harper-Collins Publishers, Inc. 1996.

Feldman, Anne. Firefighters. New York: David McKay Company, 1979.

Halberstadt, Hans. The American Fire Engine: Osceola, Wisconsin: Motorbooks International

Holzman, Robert S. The Romance of Firefighting. New York: Harper & Brothers, 1956.

Lawrence, Vera Brodsky. Music for Patriots, Politicians, and Presidents. New York: Macmillan Publishing Co, Inc., 1975.

Little, Ken and McNalis, John. History of Chicago Fire Houses of the 19th Century. Chicago, Illinois: Ken Little and John McNalis, 1996.

Lyons, Paul Robert. Fire in America. Boston, Massachusetts: National Fire Protection Association, 1976.

Morris, John V. Fires and Firefighters. New York: Bramhall House, 1955.

Smith, Dennis and Freedman, Jill. Firehouse. Garden City, New York: Doubleday and Company, 1977.

Zurier, Rebecca. The American Firehouse. New York: Abbeville Press, 1982.

Index